Making Quilts for Children

ELAINE HAMMOND

David & Charles

This book is dedicated with love and gratitude to my husband Rob as always,
Dr. Guy Busher, Professor Hugh Coakham and the staff of The Glen BUPA Hospital, Bristol.

A DAVID & CHARLES BOOK

First published in the UK in 2000
First published in paperback 2002

ISBN 0 7153 1459 9

Photography by Di Lewis and David Johnson
Book design by Jane Forster
Hand-drawn illustrations by Terry Evans
Diagrams by King & King

Printed in Italy by New Interlitho SpA
for David & Charles
Brunel House   Newton Abbot   Devon

Contents

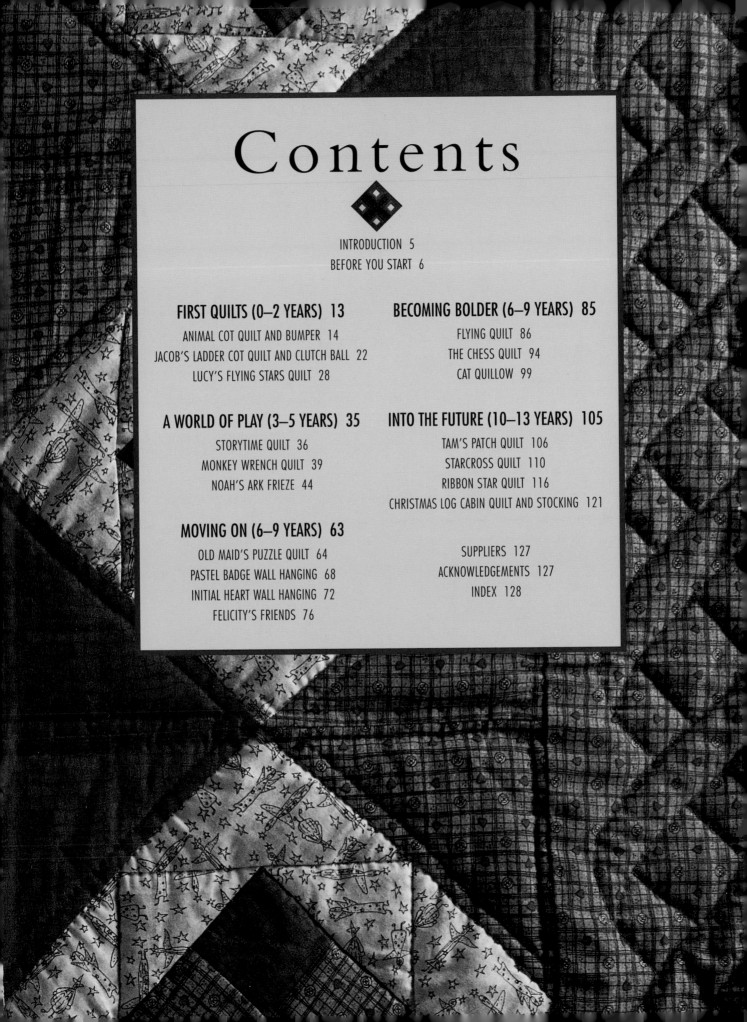

Introduction

There is something very special about designing projects for children. You can tailor the colour and style of your designs to suit a particular child's tastes and come up with something totally unique. Quilts are especially nice to give because you can enjoy snuggling in one as well as looking at it.

When I started planning this book, I thought of all the children I know and what they would like. As a result, many of the projects were shaped with a particular child in mind. Felicity's Friends, for example, grew out of a conversation I had with my niece Felicity who was feeling lonely at the time following a house move. As I developed each project further, the original germ of an idea was often replaced by fresh ideas suggested, for example, by a particular fabric.

I hope you have a lot of fun choosing the fabrics and making the quilts in this book for the children you know. Such a lovely gift is sure to be treasured for a lifetime.

Before you start

The projects in this book are easy to make if you follow the instructions. Read through this section carefully before you begin, and refer to it again as often as you need to.

Enjoy finding the fabrics for the projects you have in mind because there are so many different ones available. Remember to choose fabrics with the child in mind – perhaps you can let them help you. You will find bright colours stimulate, whilst soft colours are relaxing and soothing. Each of the projects can be made as subdued or as exciting as you wish.

MATERIALS AND EQUIPMENT

Very little equipment is required for patchwork and quilting. In both crafts the fabric is the most important ingredient, followed by the threads. Many of the gadgets you can buy are not essential, so start with the basics and gradually add more as you come across useful items.

FABRIC Most types of fabric can be used for patchwork, quilting and appliqué, however, some are easier to handle than others. Generally, you will find 100% cotton fabrics the easiest and most satisfying to work with, and they hold a crease well. Wash your fabrics separately in mild soap after buying them.

I have erred on the side of generosity when recommending fabric amounts, and I make no apology for this. Too often I have found that I am short of one vital extra piece, so now I always buy a little more. And how else can I maintain the healthy scrap bag we quilters are famous for?

THREADS For most hand sewing it is best to match the thread to the fabric used. As cotton fabric is generally used for patchwork projects, 100% cotton thread (eg Sylko 50) is best. You can buy special cotton-covered polyester threads for quilting, which are thicker and less likely to tangle: alternatively use ordinary thread pulled through beeswax to make it strong and smooth.

NEEDLES You will need a range of needles. For piecing try 'sharps'; for quilting use 'betweens'. Choose a larger size to start with (8 or 9), before changing to a finer needle as you gain more practice. Large doll-making needles help to make tacking up a quilt much easier.

PINS Use dressmaking pins to hold the fabric together when piecing or doing appliqué work. Long fine pins with glass or plastic heads are best because they are easiest to find in the fabric. On finer fabric however, you may need silk pins. Use safety pins to hold your quilt sandwich together before tacking up.

PIN CUSHION Store some pins in a pin cushion while you are working. This will help to keep them sharp and make it less likely for you to stab yourself.

THIMBLE A thimble can seem unwieldy when you first wear one, but prolonged sewing without one will soon convince you how useful it is. There are many types you can buy: find one that is comfortable and which stays on. At first it will seem strange, but you will soon forget you are wearing it.

SCISSORS Three types of scissors are required for patchwork and quilting: one for cutting paper, a large pair for cutting fabric and a small pair for trimming seam allowances and threads. Choose comfortable, sharp scissors and keep them exclusively for this type of work. They should then last for years.

ROTARY CUTTER A rotary cutter saves hours of laborious cutting with scissors and is really useful when you have dozens of fabric pieces to cut. For the best results, use a self-healing cutting mat and a rotary ruler with your rotary cutter.

SEWING MACHINE Although many patchwork projects have to be made by hand, a sewing machine is recommended for freeing you from some of the drudgery of sewing.

TEMPLATES These can be made from cardboard or plastic. Template plastic is available from patchwork suppliers (see page 127) and is best for large projects where many pieces are needed. If you are only going to use a template a few times, medium-weight card will be sufficient.

COLOURED PENCILS These are helpful for deciding colour choices and for transferring quilting designs on to fabric.

PAPER Several types are needed, including rough paper for sketching, squared paper (preferably 5mm/¼in) (see Suppliers, page 127) and graph paper, both squares and isometric.

GLUE STICK This is handy for making templates and for gluing paper sheets together to make larger areas.

WADDING (BATTING) This is available in various types – polyester, polyester/cotton, cotton and wool – and weights, from 2–6oz. You can also buy some low-loft fleeces that are less than 2oz and useful for small quilts.

QUILTING FRAMES AND HOOPS Holding the piece taut in a quilting frame or hoop will help you to achieve an even tension, and keep your stitches the same size front and back. These frames can be hand-held, floor standing or held by plastic clips.

BASIC TECHNIQUES

You will need the following basic techniques to make the quilts in this book.

ENLARGING PATTERNS

It is often necessary to enlarge patchwork patterns and this can be done on a photocopier since most machines now have percentage facilities. If you need to enlarge your design more than the maximum percentage on the photocopier, copy it once using the maximum enlargement setting, then copy your copy, enlarging it again to the correct size.

 Sometimes it is only possible to show half or quarter of a symmetrical quilting pattern. In this case you will need to enlarge the pattern as instructed and then trace it off once (for a half pattern) or three times (for a quarter pattern) before assembling the pieces to make a pattern for the whole design.

PIECING

All of the quilts in this book can be pieced by hand, however using a machine will make light work of the sewing, for example on the Monkey Wrench quilt on page 39. Whether you decide to sew your quilt by hand or machine, remember to take into account the Seam Allowance Rule.

MAKING AND USING TEMPLATES

Patchwork templates should be made from durable material because they will be reused many times on the one quilt. Store your templates in a clear plastic grip-seal bag, marking the name and size of the block.

To make a template in plastic Place the plastic over the template shape and, trace off the relevant outlines using a ruler and fine marker pen, making sure the corners are clearly marked and taking into account the Seam Allowance Rule. Mark the straight grain, number or letter, the name of the block, where possible, and 1 of 5, 2 of 5, and so on, where relevant. Then cut out the shape using sharp scissors, a craft knife or rotary cutter.

To make a template in card Trace your design onto paper. Glue this to medium-weight card. Then cut out the shape using sharp scissors.

SEAM ALLOWANCE RULE

Most of the templates in this book are marked with an inner (sewing) line and an outer (cutting) line that includes a seam allowance.

 When you cut the templates for machine piecing you should include the seam allowances, cutting the templates to the outer line. The width of the sewing machine foot will automatically allow 5mm (¼in) between the cut edge and the sewing line. Check the width of your presser foot to make sure of this.

 For hand piecing or hand appliqué, the seam allowances should *not* be included on the template. Cut them out to the inner line. Place the template on the fabric and draw around it. This drawn line becomes the sewing line. Cut out the fabric piece allowing a 5mm (¼in) seam allowance from the drawn line. You will be surprised by how quickly you can learn to do this by eye.

MARKING AND CUTTING FABRIC

Many of the templates in this book have an arrowed line on them. When placing the template on to your fabric, make sure that the arrowed line runs parallel to the straight grain of the fabric. The straight grain runs parallel to the selvage (the neatened edge of the fabric). If you don't follow the straight grain as directed, the patchwork pieces may distort as you sew them.

ROTARY CUTTING

There is no doubt that rotary cutters have drastically reduced the time spent on cutting. To use a rotary cutter, press your fabrics and layer them, either as several pieces together or as one piece folded into four to six layers. Place your ruler on top and, pressing firmly on your ruler with one hand to keep it stable, cut along the ruler edge with the cutter. Press fairly hard and push the blade away from you. A rotary cutter blade is very sharp so you must replace the guard each time you use it.

ASSEMBLING A BLOCK

It is helpful to pin your pieces onto a polystyrene board, especially when the patchwork block is made up of many pieces. As you finish piecing each unit of the block, pin it back into place on the board, so you can see the progress.

If you are piecing by hand, use running stitches with an occasional backstitch (about every 2cm/¾in) to give extra strength.

Unlike dressmaking, when you press the seams open in patchwork you press the seam to one side, usually towards the darker fabric. In this way, the seams are stronger and less visible on the right side.

MACHINE PIECING

Machine piecing is a valid part of the craft of patchwork today whatever the purists may say. For quilts that are going to take a lot of wear and tear or that have to be made in a hurry, you cannot beat machine piecing. Follow the rules below to make the whole process quicker and easier and avoid unwanted unpicking.

◆ Get to know your sewing machine. Study the manual and see what special facilities it has. Practise on spare fabric and learn to control the machine automatically so you don't have to worry about your foot. Make sure it is cleaned and oiled regularly, especially before and after a heavy sewing session.

◆ Prepare for work. Make sure you are comfortable. Wind plenty of bobbins in a neutral or complementary colour before you start, so you don't have to keep stopping. It is important also to make a practice block before you start a marathon piecing session to check that you have got it right. Press this block then measure it to be sure it is coming up to the size it should.

◆ Machine piecing *always* requires a 5mm (¼in) seam allowance, so check that your machine has a foot that is exactly this width before you start.

◆ Cut accurately. You do not need to mark the sewing line for machine piecing (see Seam Allowance Rule, page 7), but it is very important that you cut accurately.

THE QUILTING PROCESS

Once the patchwork blocks have been pieced together, you will need to quilt together the pieced quilt top and the wadding (batting) and backing fabric. All the quilts in this book with the exception of the Ribbon Quilt were quilted by hand.

The quilting process begins with preparations for quilting, including marking out a design, tacking up or sandwiching the quilt layers, followed by the actual quilting. Unless you are intending to outline quilt, quilt 'in the ditch' or tie the layers together (see opposite) you will first need to mark out your quilting pattern onto your quilt top.

MARKING OUT A DESIGN

See page 7 for advice on enlarging and tracing the quilting pattern. Press your top fabric layer well and lay it on a flat surface ready for you to mark out your quilting design using one of the following methods.

◆ The easiest method is to tape your design to a light box, well-lit window or glass-topped table with a lamp underneath it. The light will show through even dark fabrics. Using masking tape, tape your fabric on top of the design and then mark the design with pencil or water-erasable marker.

◆ Use coloured pencils (dark for light fabrics and light for dark fabrics) to draw around your template or use a ruler for straight lines. You can also use a water-erasable marker for this.

TACKING UP

Before tacking up, make sure both your top and backing layers are well pressed as it will not be possible to do it after quilting. To tack (baste) up, or make a quilt sandwich, place the backing fabric right side down on a flat surface (usually the floor), then add the wadding (batting) well smoothed out and finally the quilt top with the right side uppermost. Tack (baste) the layers from the top. Work lines of tacking from the middle towards the edges, to form a grid pattern. It is important to tack (baste) the layers together firmly to prevent them shifting as you quilt, especially if you do not intend to use a frame or a hoop. If you are using a frame, place the work in it after tacking up.

QUILTING

The quilting stitch is an evenly spaced running stitch that should appear the same on both sides of the work. It is more important that the stitches are even than small, and you will soon find your own personal tension. Begin at the centre of the work and piece outwards.

To begin the thread make a quilter's knot (see opposite) and insert the needle about 12mm (½in) away from the start of the design and bring it up in the right place to start. Give a slight, sharp tug and the knot will pop between the layers to lose itself in the wadding (batting).

To fasten off take a small backstitch through the wadding (batting) and quilt top only. Pierce this backstitch with the point of the needle (to anchor it) and run the thread off into the wadding (batting) before snipping off the thread.

MAKING A QUILTER'S KNOT

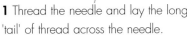
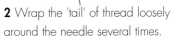

1 Thread the needle and lay the long 'tail' of thread across the needle.

2 Wrap the 'tail' of thread loosely around the needle several times.

3 Pull the needle gently through the thread and a flat knot will be formed.

OUTLINE QUILTING

This is often used with patchwork, especially if the pieced work is intricate. The quilting is worked approximately 5mm (¼in) away from the patchwork seams, holding the layers together and enhancing the patchwork effect.

QUILTING 'IN THE DITCH'

This type of quilting can also be done by machine and is used to complement a patchwork design when extra lines of stitching are not desired but the quilt layers still need to be held together. The stitching is done with a toning thread in the seam line where the pieces have been joined.

TYING

If working on a thickly padded item, such as the Jacob's Ladder quilt on page 22, it is often easier to hold the layers together by tying. The knots are formed about 15cm (6in) apart, by taking a stitch and making a reef knot as shown below.

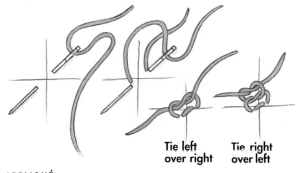

Tie left over right   **Tie right over left**

APPLIQUÉ

Appliqué involves laying and attaching one piece of fabric over another to create a decorative design. It is attached in the following ways:

BLANKET STITCH APPLIQUÉ

Blanket stitch is used around the edges of an appliqué motif to enhance the design and cover raw edges (therefore no seam allowances are needed). It is used to attach the felt pieces in the Noah's Ark frieze on page 44.

OVER PAPERS APPLIQUÉ

In this type of appliqué the motif is traced onto paper, with no seam allowances. The fabric is then cut out, allowing for a 5mm (¼in) seam allowance. Place the paper on the wrong side of fabric and pull the seam allowance over towards the paper, clipping corners and curves where necessary. Tack (baste) the fabric all round then sew to the background fabric using hem stitch. This method is also used in the Noah's Ark frieze.

BINDING

Most of the quilts in this book are finished off with bias binding. This can be bought or made from leftover scraps of fabric. The binding is added around the edges of the quilt sandwich and encases all the layers. Usually the first fold is sewn in place by machine, then the binding is pulled over to the back and hemstitched into place.

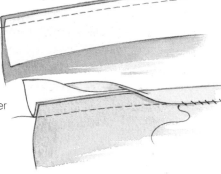

FINISHING CORNERS

Mitring is the neatest way to finish the corners on a quilt border. Place one border piece over the other, then using a pencil and ruler, draw a line from the quilt corner to the overlap corner as shown below. Swap the uppermost corner and draw the same line. Using the lines as sewing guides, pin and sew from innermost to the outer corner. Trim away the seam allowance, leaving 5mm (¼in), then press.

STITCH LIBRARY

All the stitches you will require to make the projects in this book are described below.

BACKSTITCH

This is a linear stitch which appears as a continuous line of small stitches. Bring the needle up through the front of the fabric at 1, down at 2 (which should be next to the last stitch) and up at 3.

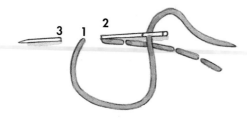

BLANKET STITCH

This is a variable and useful stitch which can be worked with different densities of stitches and with varying stitch lengths. Bring the thread out on the lower line shown in the diagram. Re-insert the needle at 1 on the upper line and out again at 2, with the thread under the needle point so that a loop is formed.

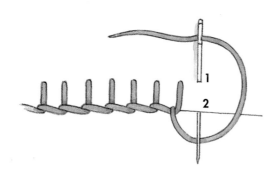

CHICKEN SCRATCH QUILTING

Chicken scratch quilting is an unusual way to fasten three layers of backing, wadding and top fabric together. Bring the needle up through the fabric at 1, take it across and down at 2. Run the thread across the back of the fabric and up at 3. Stitch down through the fabric at 4. Run the thread behind the fabric and up at 5 and repeat.

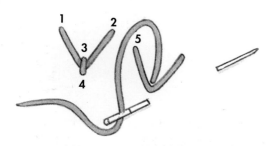

FEATHER STITCH

This is a decorative stitch which is worked from the top down. It is an ideal stitch to cover seams or edges of appliqué. Bring the needle up through the fabric at 1, take the needle down at 2, and back out at 3, and so on.

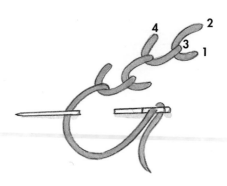

FRENCH KNOT

Bring the thread up through the fabric at the point where you want the French knot to be and hold it down with your thumb. Twist the thread around the needle twice, then insert the needle back into the fabric beside the point where it first emerged.

HEM STITCH

Make a small vertical stitch to start, going from 1 to 3 as shown on the diagram. Bring the needle out at 1, in at 2, out at 3 and back in at 4. Bring the needle down horizontally to start another stitch.

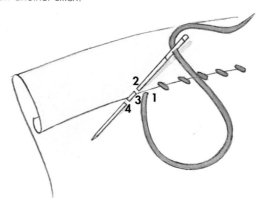

OVERSEWING

This is a method of attaching two pieces of fabric together, commonly used in hand piecing for patchwork. Simply take small stitches through both layers of the fabric, working along the line to be stitched.

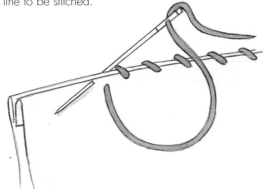

QUILTING STITCH

The quilting stitch is basically a small, neat running stitch, with the thread being passed under and over the fabric. Bring the needle out to the front of the fabric at 1 and insert it at 2. Bring the needle out at 3 and repeat.

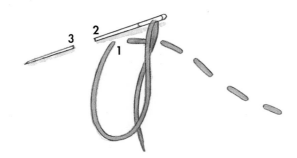

SATIN STITCH

This is a long, smooth stitch which covers the fabric well and is a good filling-in stitch. Straight stitches (see below) are worked closely together across the shape to be embroidered, with care taken to maintain a neat edge. Avoid making the stitches too long. Bring the needle out to the front of the fabric at 1. Insert it at 2 and then bring it out again at 3, and so on.

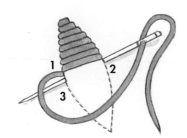

STEM STITCH

This stitch is used for outlines, flower stems and so on, and can be used as a filling stitch. Work from left to right, taking small, regular stitches along the line of the design. The thread should always emerge on the left side of the previous stitch. Bring the needle out to the front of the fabric at 1. Insert it at 2 and bring it out again at 3, and so on.

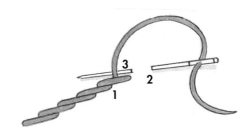

STRAIGHT STITCH

This stitch can be worked either regularly or irregularly. The stitches can be of various sizes but should not be too long or loose. Bring the needle out to the front of the fabric at 1. Insert it at 2 and out again at 3, and so on.

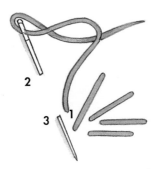

A detail from one of the pages of the Noah's Ark frieze, page 44: stem stitch is used to highlight the snail's shell.

First
Quilts

Welcome a new arrival with a beautiful handmade quilt. There are three designs to choose from: a fun Animal cot quilt with a matching cot bumper that holds soft toys for amusing a wakeful infant; a bright Jacob's Ladder cot quilt with a clutch ball made from the leftover fabric, and the pretty pastel shades of Lucy's Flying Stars quilt.

0–2 years

ANIMAL COT QUILT AND BUMPER

I found this delightful quilt at an American quilt festival. It was made in the 1920s and was extremely worn, but very soft. It is lovely to think of generations of babies being wrapped in it. Now you can make the same quilt in crisp new fabrics as a family heirloom. The animals look as if they are pieced in squares, but in fact they are appliquéd, with the quilting forming a grid over each one. I liked the animals so much that I made four of them again as soft toys with a matching cot bumper to hold them.

FINISHED SIZE
132 x 92cm (52 x 36in)

YOU WILL NEED
- White fabric, 5.25m (5¼yds) by 90cm (36in) or 112cm (44in) wide
- Pastel fabrics for the animals, approx. 25cm (¼yd) each
- Wadding (batting), one 94 x 135cm (37 x 53in) piece for the cot quilt; two strips, one 28 x 214cm (11 x 84in) and one 14 x 214cm (5½ x 84in) for the cot bumper
- Stranded cotton (floss)
- Toy stuffing
- White quilting thread
- Blue bias binding, 16m (16yds) by 2.5cm (1in) wide

Fabric quantities include the cot bumper and toys

NOTE BEFORE BEGINNING
The patterns for the appliqué animals are given on a grid. Each square on the grid represents 2.5cm (1in). Copy each design onto 2.5cm (1in) squared paper and colour it in as shown on the appliqué templates on pages 19–21. Photocopy your redrawn shapes and stick them to cardboard. Use this to cut out templates for the animals remembering to allow for a 5mm (¼in) seam allowance.

TO MAKE THE QUILT

1 Cut a 135cm (53in) length of white fabric and lay it to one side for the quilt backing.

2 Cut a second 135cm (53in) length of white fabric for the quilt top. Press.

3 Referring to the quilting and piecing diagram on page 17, mark the quilting pattern onto the quilt top. For the animal squares make a grid template from graph paper remembering that each square represents 2.5cm (1in). For the border, photocopy the quilting pattern on page 16 enlarging by 125%. You may find it helpful to go over the photocopied lines again with a fine permanent marker. To transfer the quilting patterns onto the fabric, work on a flat surface and use a water-erasable marker. Now mark the outlines of the appliqué animals onto each of the gridded squares.

4 Make the animals one by one: the cat or the rabbit is the easiest to start with. Cut out all the pieces from your fabrics, leaving a 5mm (¼in) seam allowance for stitching and turning.

5 Following the appliqué templates, pages 17–19, as a pattern, attach the paws, ears, tails, etc to the animal bodies with a seam using running stitch. Some small pieces, such as the rooster's feet, will need to be appliquéd directly onto the quilt top separately. Turn under a 5mm (¼in) hem on all the raw edges, and tack (baste) down.

6 Using the grid marked earlier, pin the appliqué animals in place on the quilt top fabric and hem stitch in position.

7 Finish off the animals by using stranded cotton (floss) to embroider the eyes and other details marked on the appliqué templates on pages

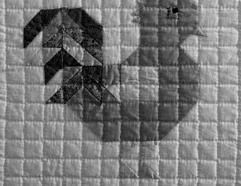

BORDER QUILTING PATTERN: ENLARGE BY 125%

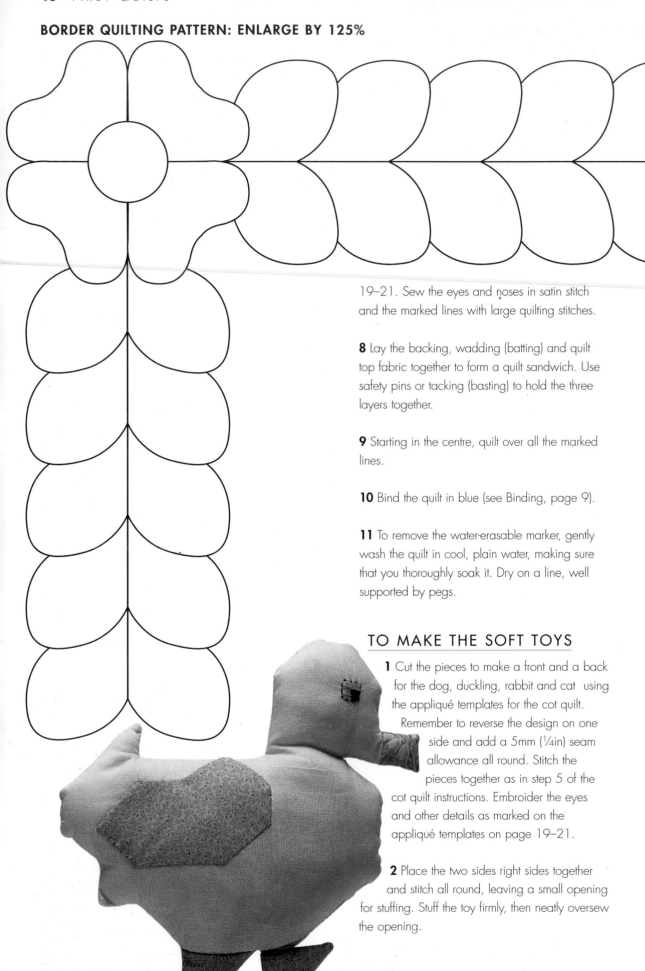

19–21. Sew the eyes and noses in satin stitch and the marked lines with large quilting stitches.

8 Lay the backing, wadding (batting) and quilt top fabric together to form a quilt sandwich. Use safety pins or tacking (basting) to hold the three layers together.

9 Starting in the centre, quilt over all the marked lines.

10 Bind the quilt in blue (see Binding, page 9).

11 To remove the water-erasable marker, gently wash the quilt in cool, plain water, making sure that you thoroughly soak it. Dry on a line, well supported by pegs.

TO MAKE THE SOFT TOYS

1 Cut the pieces to make a front and a back for the dog, duckling, rabbit and cat using the appliqué templates for the cot quilt. Remember to reverse the design on one side and add a 5mm (¼in) seam allowance all round. Stitch the pieces together as in step 5 of the cot quilt instructions. Embroider the eyes and other details as marked on the appliqué templates on page 19–21.

2 Place the two sides right sides together and stitch all round, leaving a small opening for stuffing. Stuff the toy firmly, then neatly oversew the opening.

QUILTING AND PIECING DIAGRAM

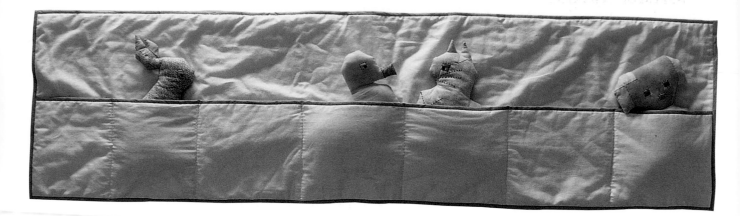

TO MAKE THE COT BUMPER

1 Fold the remaining white fabric in half length-ways and cut down the fold to make two pieces A and B.

2 Fold piece B in half lengthways and cut down the fold. Discard one half. Fold the remaining half in half again lengthways and cut along the fold. You now have two strips 14cm (5½in) wide by 2.3m (2½yds) long. Place the narrower length of wadding (batting) between these two strips. Pin the three layers together with safety pins. Bind one long edge with the bias binding.

3 Fold piece A in half again lengthways and cut along the fold. You now have two strips of fabric 28cm (11in) wide by 2.3m (2½yds) long. Place the wider length of wadding (batting) between these two strips. Pin the three layers together with safety pins. Bind one long edge with bias binding.

4 Lay the wider strip flat on a surface. Place the narrower strip on top matching all the raw edges at the bottom. Pin the two short edges and the bottom edge together through all the layers.

5 Divide the bumper into seven equal segments. Mark with lines of tacking (basting) from the bottom edge to the binding. Quilt along these lines to form the pockets.

6 Now bind the long bottom edge and the two short edges.

7 Cut eight 61cm (24in) lengths of bias binding for the ties. Fold each piece in half lengthways, turn in the ends and machine stitch or oversew down the long edge. Fold each tie in half and firmly stitch to the bumper where it will fit to the corners of the cot.

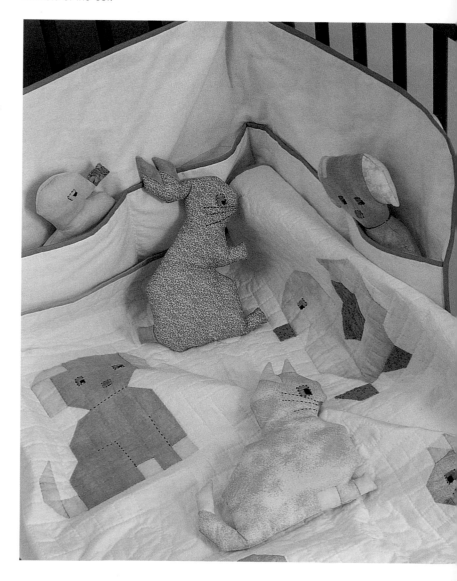

APPLIQUÉ TEMPLATES

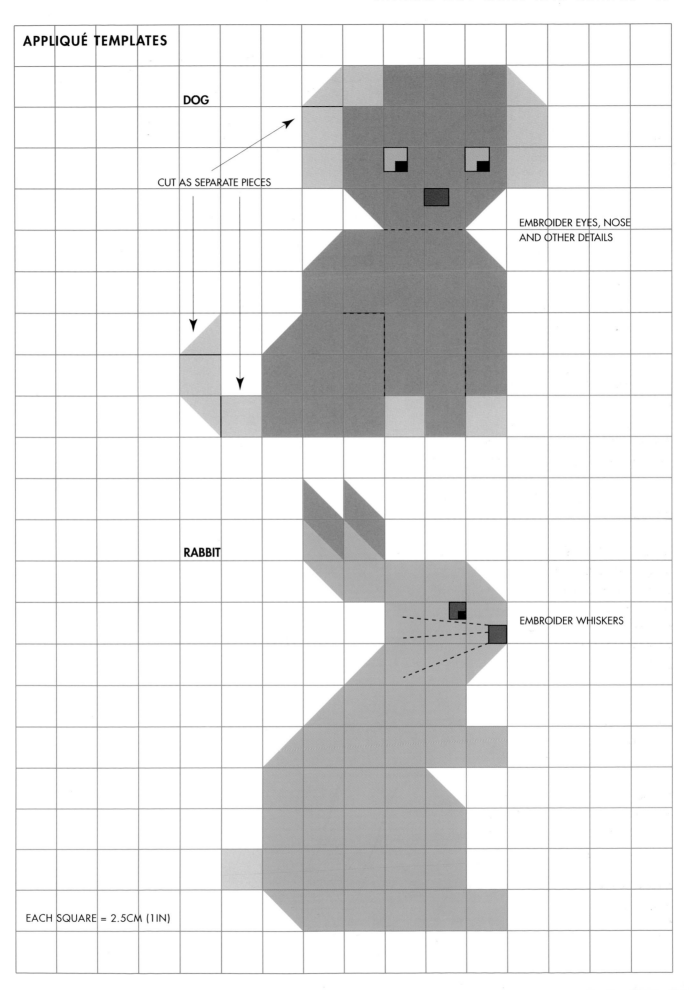

DOG

CUT AS SEPARATE PIECES

EMBROIDER EYES, NOSE AND OTHER DETAILS

RABBIT

EMBROIDER WHISKERS

EACH SQUARE = 2.5CM (1IN)

APPLIQUÉ TEMPLATES

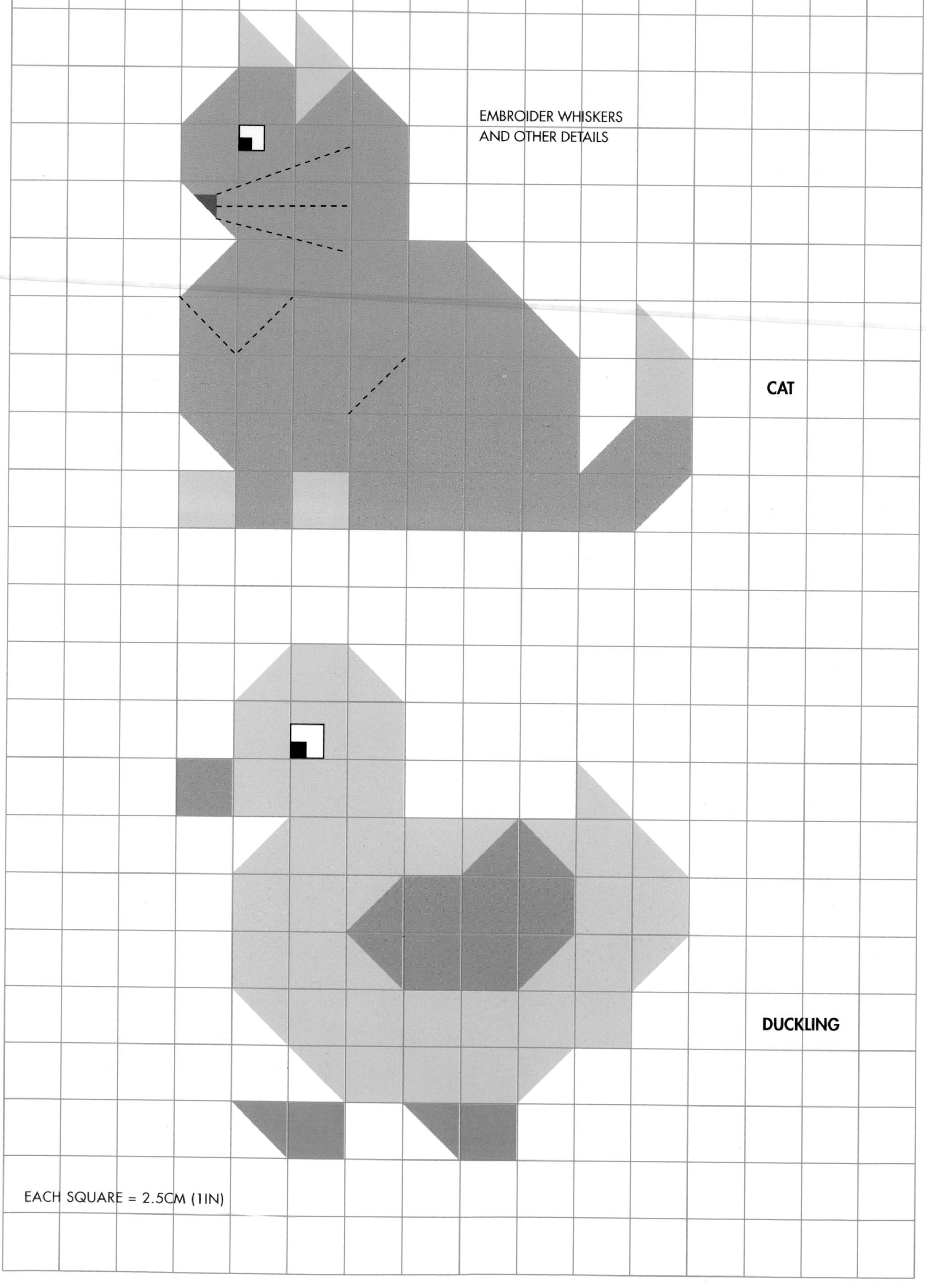

EMBROIDER WHISKERS
AND OTHER DETAILS

CAT

DUCKLING

EACH SQUARE = 2.5CM (1IN)

APPLIQUÉ TEMPLATES

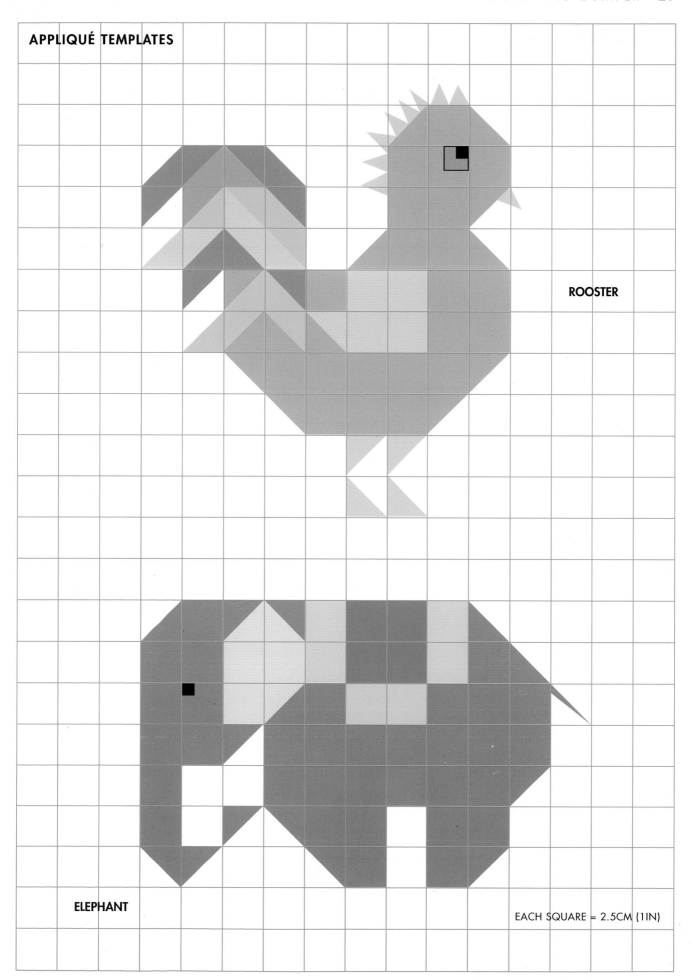

ROOSTER

ELEPHANT

EACH SQUARE = 2.5CM (1IN)

JACOB'S LADDER COT QUILT AND CLUTCH BALL

The name for the block on this quilt comes from the Bible story of Jacob's vision of a ladder leading up to Heaven. I chose bright primary colours that will stimulate a toddler. My patterned fabric has tropical fishes on it, but there are many other lovely prints to choose from. If you are decorating a child's room, you could make this quilt the central focus for the room. This is a generous sized cot quilt, which will also fit a bed later on. I used up the leftover fabric to make a clutch ball for a toddler.

FINISHED SIZE
158 x 112cm (62 x 44in)

BLOCK SIZE
23cm (9in) square

YOU WILL NEED
- Main patterned fabric, 1m (1yd) by 112cm (44in) wide for the blocks and borders
- Three other fabrics, 75cm (¾yd) each by 112cm (44in) wide
- Backing fabric, 2m (2yds) by 112cm (44in) wide
- Wadding (batting), 115 x 160cm (45x63in)
- Bias binding, 6m (6yds) by 2.5cm (1in) wide
- Stranded cotton (floss) in four matching colours for tying the quilt

TO MAKE THE QUILT

1 Wash and press all the fabrics. Cut two 9 x 152.4cm (3½ x 60in) pieces and two 9 x 91.5cm (3½ x 36in) pieces from the main fabric for the quilt borders. Join the strips to make the appropriate length if necessary. Trace off and make Templates A, B and C on page 24 (see Seam Allowance Rule, page 7). Cut out the following pieces from your fabrics (see Rotary Cutting, page 7):

    96 x Template A in yellow
    96 x Template A in main fabric (blue print)
    240 x Template B in red
    240 x Template B in turquoise
    20 x Template C in each of red, yellow and turquoise

2 Join each of the red B pieces to a turquoise B piece along one side with a 5mm (¼in) seam. Sew these together in pairs to form a series of squares (the B squares). Join each of the yellow A pieces to a blue print A piece along the diagonal to make the A squares.

A SQUARE

B SQUARE

BLOCK PIECING DIAGRAM

QUILT TEMPLATES

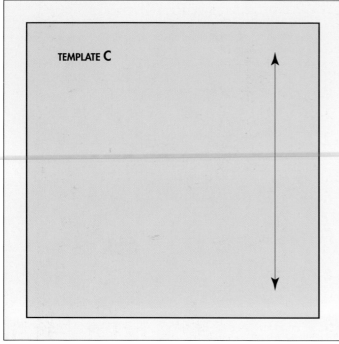

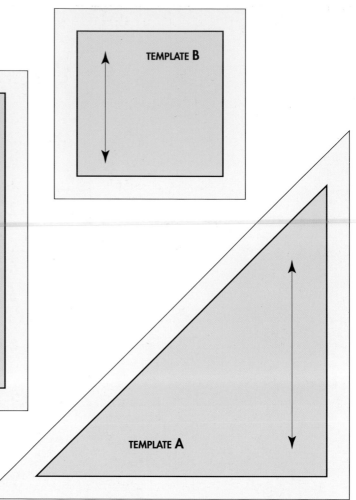

3 Sew the A and B squares together to make three strips as shown: use one B square, one A square and one B square for the first and third strips, and one A square, one B square and one A square for the second strip.

4 Join these three strips together to make a block (see the block piecing diagram on page 22). Make up another 23 blocks in this way.

5 Sew the blocks together using the quilt piecing diagram opposite as a guide. Rotate half of the blocks by 90° to form a diamond pattern. Press the quilt top.

6 Fold each C piece in half then fold in the two short edges to form a triangle and press.

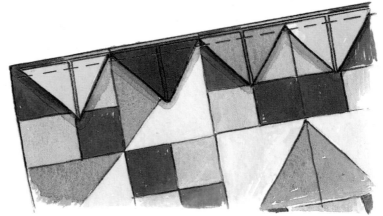

7 Pin the triangles right sides together along the quilt top 25mm (1/8in) away from the edge. Stitch into place. Fold and pin the triangles along the three other edges of the quilt in the same way.

8 Pin the top and bottom border pieces right sides together over the triangles along the top edge of the quilt and sew together using a 5mm (1/4in) seam allowance. Do the same with the side

QUILT PIECING DIAGRAM

border pieces, extending across the top and bottom borders.

9 Press the completed quilt top. Lay the backing, wadding (batting) and quilt top together to form a quilt sandwich. Use safety pins or tacking (basting) to hold the three layers together.

10 Thread a large needle with two strands of each of the stranded cotton colours. Quilt the three layers together by 'tying' them at the corners of the red and turquoise blocks (see Tying, page 9).

11 Bind the quilt using the bias binding (see Binding, page 9).

TO MAKE THE CLUTCH BALL

A Victorian pin cushion design has been adapted to create soft, safe toys. Templates are given for three sizes: the largest has been made into a clutch ball using the same fabrics as the Jacob's Ladder cot quilt; the middle size is ideal for hanging on a pram; while the smallest one makes a lovely Christmas tree ornament.

1 Trace the two templates opposite using the curved line C and make cardboard templates for your clutch ball.

2 Cut out 12 x Template 1 in yellow and 12 x Template 2 in blue print. Do not add a seam allowance.

3 Fold one of the yellow pieces right sides together and sew along the straight edge using a 5mm (¼in) seam allowance and leaving a gap for turning.

4 Take a blue piece and lay it flat with right sides together against the open curved edge of the yellow piece. Pin carefully into place using a 5mm (¼in) seam allowance. Stitch all round the edge to form a segment. If sewing by hand use backstitch to make the seam strong.

5 Turn the segment to the right side through the gap in the straight edge, and smooth the seams using a knitting needle or plastic swizzle stick. Stuff the segment carefully and not too firmly, easing the stuffing into the corners. Oversew the gap closed. Make the rest of the segments in the same way.

6 Join two segments together at the yellow point with a button bar. Thread your needle with stranded cotton (floss) and knot the end. Push it into the segment about 5mm (¼in) away from the corner, bring the tip out again at the corner and pull the thread so that the knot is hidden in the stuffing. Take a small backstitch, then take a stitch into the corner of the next segment. Work several long stitches between the two segments, then secure them with a small stitch. Now work button-hole stitch over the bar from left to right. This will make a good strong join.

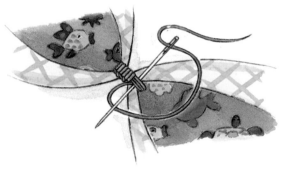

7 Stitch all the segments together in pairs in this way. Twist two pairs of segments together as shown below. Join the twisted pairs with more buttonhole bars on the outer edges of the ball.

CLUTCH BALL TEMPLATES

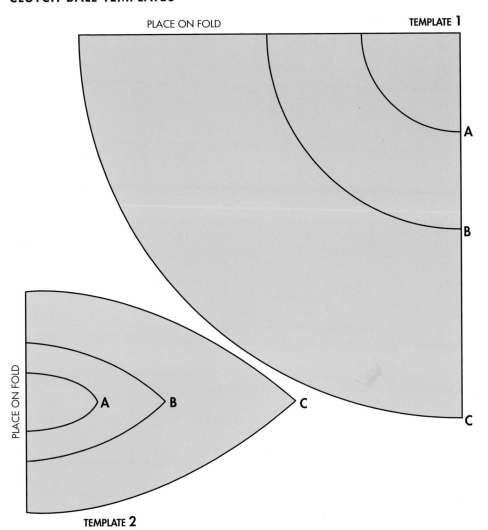

PLACE ON FOLD

TEMPLATE **1**

A

B

PLACE ON FOLD

A   B   C

C

C

TEMPLATE **2**

You can use the clutch ball templates to make three different sized balls:

A = Small: 8cm (3¼in) in diameter;

B = Medium: 14cm (5½in) in diameter;

C = Large: 20cm (8in) in diameter.

Add a 25mm (⅛in) seam allowance for the smallest template (A), but no seam allowance for B and C.

LUCY'S FLYING STARS QUILT

I designed this cot quilt for my god-daughter Lucy when she was a baby. The soft pastel colours make it an ideal gift for a precious newborn, and the star design is sure to be appreciated by a growing child, too. Lucy is now eight, but her quilt is still much loved and used. The basic block for the quilt is an asymmetrical design. The star design comes alive by rotating the blocks in a group of four before they are joined together.

FINISHED SIZE 152 x 104cm (60 x 41in)
BLOCK SIZE 21.6cm (8.5in)

YOU WILL NEED

◆ Blue fabric, 1.25m (1¼yds) by 112cm (44in) wide for the blocks
◆ Pink fabric, 2.5m (2½yds) by 112cm (44in) wide for the blocks and binding
◆ Yellow fabric, 50cm (½yd) by 112cm (44in) wide for the stars
◆ Multi-print fabric, 3.25m (3¼yds) by 112cm (44in) wide for the blocks, borders and backing
◆ 2oz wadding (batting), 157 x 109cm (62 x 43in)
◆ White quilting thread

1 Wash and press all the fabrics.

2 Cut six 112 x 7.6cm (44 x 3½in) strips from the multi-print fabric for the borders and one piece 2m (2yds) long by the width of the fabric for the backing. Trace off and make Templates A–E on page 31 (see Seam Allowance Rule, page 7). Cut out the following pieces (see Rotary Cutting, on page 7):

   24 x Template A in multi-print
   24 x Template E in multi-print
   48 x Template A in blue
   24 x Template D in blue
   48 x Template B in pink
   48 x Template A in pink
   24 x Template C in pink
   24 x Template A in yellow.

EXPLODED BLOCK PIECING DIAGRAM

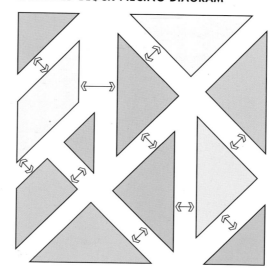

3 Construct the first block following the exploded block piecing diagram (right) and using a 5mm (¼in) seam allowance throughout. Join the pieces following the numbered order shown on the exploded block piecing diagram. Make 23 further blocks in the same way.

4 Lay all the blocks out flat and assemble the quilt following the quilt piecing diagram on page 30. Join four blocks at a time, rotating each one by a quarter turn so that a star is formed. Join all the blocks together.

QUILT PIECING DIAGRAM

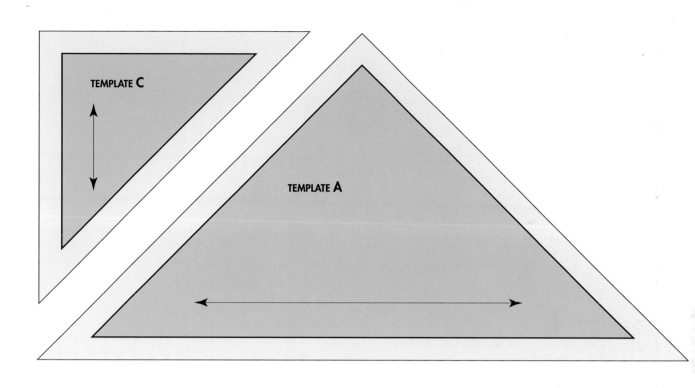

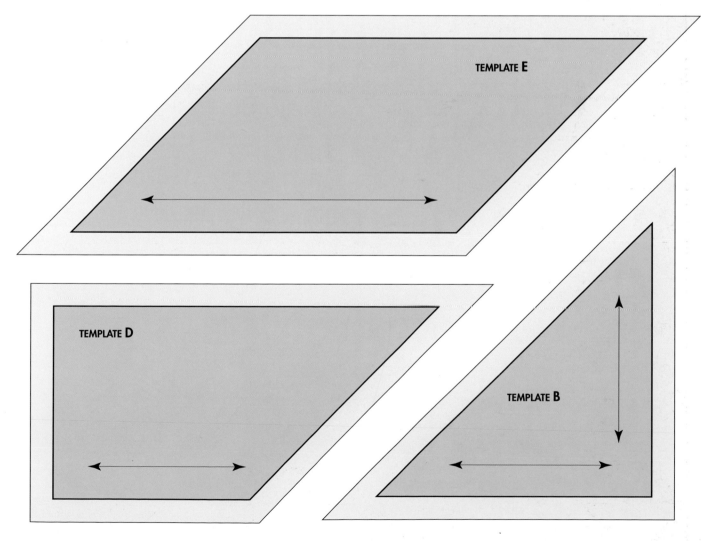

QUILTING PATTERN

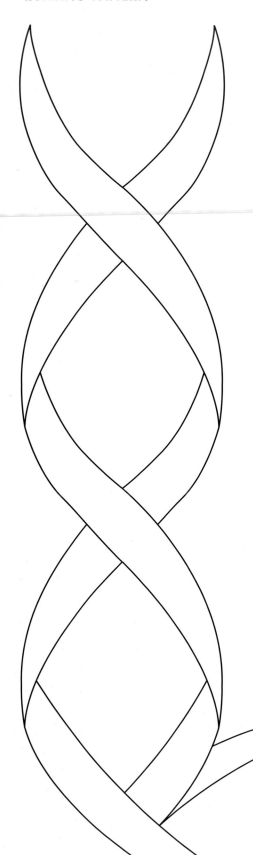

5 Join two of the border strips along one short edge and press. Repeat with two more of the strips.

6 Fold the pieced top into quarters and mark the folds. Pin one of the joined border strips to one long edge of the quilt matching the seam to the marked fold and with right sides together. Sew the border in place using a 5mm (¼in) seam allowance. Pin and sew the second joined strip to the other long edge, and the two remaining strips to the top and bottom of the quilt. Join the corners of the border and press the finished quilt top.

7 Mark out the quilting pattern on the border. Mark out a series of letters and numbers randomly on the quilt top which spell out the child's name and birthday. Take these from an alphabet in a book or on a computer and enlarge them on a photocopier. Make sure they are evenly spaced and facing in all directions to create a balanced look.

8 Lay the backing, wadding (batting) and pieced top together to form a quilt sandwich. Use safety pins or tacking (basting) to hold the three layers together.

9 Quilt around all the letters and numbers and along the border.

10 Bind the quilt using 2.5cm (1in) strips cut from the remaining pink fabric (see Binding, page 9).

A World
of Play

In this section you will find three quilts
designed to enhance the bedtime stories
children of this age love so much. There's a
bright and colourful Monkey Wrench quilt
for a little boy's first bed; a very special
appliquéd frieze that tells the story of
Noah's Ark, and the Storytime quilt, a
hand-pieced scrap quilt made from wonderful
print fabrics that will fascinate a child.

3–5 years

STORYTIME QUILT

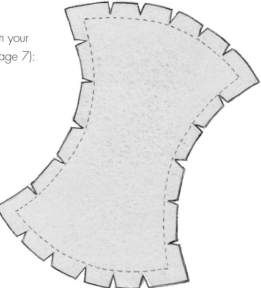

Scrap quilts, where many different fabrics are used in one quilt, have long been popular with quilters: what better use, after all, for the leftovers from your other quilting projects? Many scrap quilt designs use just one template – a triangle, a hexagon or, as in this design, the applecore. It seemed to me that putting many prints in a quilt was a good way to stimulate conversation between parent and child, and the Storytime quilt will provide ample opportunity to construct impromptu stories from the different printed fabrics chosen. Although this quilt can be sewn on a machine, I found it easier to sew by hand.

FINISHED SIZE
198cm x 162.5cm (78 x 64in)

YOU WILL NEED
- 5mm (¼in) squared gingham in the following colours – lilac and yellow, 25cm (¼yd) of each
- 5mm (¼in) squared gingham in the following colours – pink, light blue, red, navy, orange and green, 50cm (½yd) of each
- Scraps of different print fabrics
- Scraps of plain fabrics
- One metre (1yd) each of four fabrics for backing
- 2oz wadding (batting), 203 x 168cm (80 x 66in)
- Yellow quilting thread
- Yellow bias binding, 9m (9yds) by 2.5cm (1in) wide

A 5mm (¼in) seam allowance is used throughout

1 Wash and press all the fabrics.

2 Make a template from the Applecore Template on page 38. All the pieces in this quilt are cut from the one template, so it is advisable to make this template from plastic because a cardboard one will wear down too quickly (see Making and Using Templates, page 7). Carefully cut the notches marked on the template.

3 Mark and cut the following pieces from your fabrics (see the Seam Allowance Rule, page 7):
  6 x lilac and yellow gingham
  14 x pink and light blue gingham
  26 x red and navy gingham
  36 x orange and green gingham
  118 x different print fabrics
  114 x plain fabrics
There should be a total of 396 pieces in this quilt.

4 Clip the curves on each piece as shown in the diagram, right, to help with piecing.

Scrap quilts are an excellent way to use up leftover fabric from other quilts. Using only prints, however, would be too overpowering so I included as many pieces in plain fabrics and gingham to tone them down. Make a photocopy of the quilt piecing diagram opposite to help you keep track of your piecing.

QUILT PIECING DIAGRAM

KEY White applecores = picture fabrics
Coloured applecores = plain fabrics
Squared applecores = gingham fabrics

APPLECORE TEMPLATE

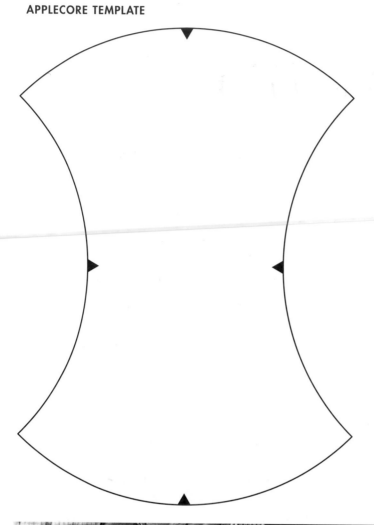

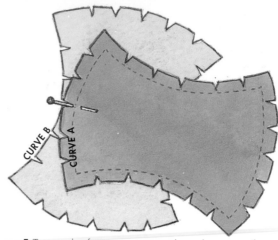

5 To join the first two pieces, place the point of a pin through the notch on curve A on one piece and through the notch on curve B on the second piece as shown above. Pin the rest of the curve in a 5mm (¼in) seam, stretching the fabric slightly to fit. Stitch the seam, using running stitch with the occasional backstitch. Add the next piece at right angles in the same way.

6 Join the pieces in this way until you have pieced the whole quilt. Refer to a photocopy of the quilt piecing diagram on page 39 while you are working to keep track of your piecing. I began by piecing the lilac and yellow gingham pieces in the centre, then joined more pieces into strips and sewed these around the centre.

7 Press the quilt top when all the piecing is complete.

8 Join the four fabrics to create the backing, and press the seams open.

9 Lay the backing face down and put the wadding (batting) and pieced quilt on top to form a quilt sandwich. Use safety pins or tacking (basting) to hold the three layers together.

10 Working by eye, quilt following the shape of each applecore piece 5mm (¼in) from the edge, with the exception of the outer border which will be bound and therefore does not need quilting.

11 Bind the quilt with the bias binding (see Binding, page 9). You can stretch the binding slightly to fit the curves.

12 Sign and date your quilt.

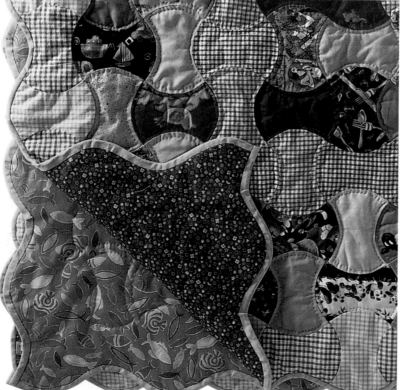

MONKEY WRENCH QUILT

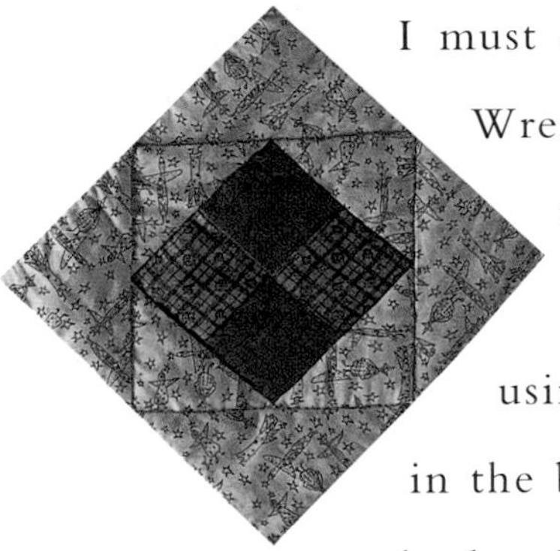

I must confess I don't know why this block is called Monkey Wrench, but it did occur to me while I was making the quilt that there could be a link here with cheeky monkeys. And here is an ideal design to make for a little boy using bold, strong colours. It's also one of the easiest quilts in the book – it can be machine pieced in no time and quilted by hand or by machine.

FINISHED SIZE
234 x 173cm (92 x 68in)
BLOCK SIZE 30cm (12in)

YOU WILL NEED
◆ Red fabric, 1.5m (1½yds) by 112cm (44in) wide
◆ Blue fabric, 1.5m (1½yds) by 112cm (44in) wide
◆ Yellow fabric, 50cm (½yd) by 112cm (44in) wide
◆ Backing fabric, 6m (6yds) by 112cm (44in) wide
◆ 2oz wadding (batting), 240 x 180cm (94 x 71in)
◆ Red quilting thread

A 5mm (¼in) seam allowance is used throughout

1 Wash and press all the fabrics. Cut two 234 x 15cm (92 x 6in) strips, one in red and one in blue, and two 178 x 15cm (70 x 6in) strips, one in red and one in blue for the border. Trace off and make Templates A–D on page 43 (see Seam Allowance Rule, page 7). Cut out the following pieces from your fabrics (see Rotary Cutting, page 7, and Machine Piecing, page 8):

    70 x Template A in blue
    70 x Template A in red
    140 x Template B in yellow
    140 x Template C in yellow
    70 x Template D in red
    70 x Template D in blue

If you want your quilt to appeal to a little girl instead of a little boy, make your quilt in pastel coloured fabrics instead of bold ones.

EXPLODED BLOCK PIECING DIAGRAM

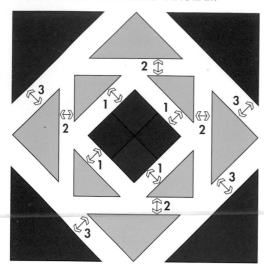

2 Make the first block following the numbered sequence in the exploded block piecing diagram above. Sew a red D piece to a blue D piece. Repeat. Press the seams and sew the two strips right sides together to form the centre of the block. Sew a yellow C piece to each side of the square (1 on the diagram) and press. Sew a yellow B piece to each side of the square (2) and press. Sew two red A pieces and two blue A pieces to opposite sides of the square (3). Press the completed block.

3 Make 34 more blocks in this way.

4 Join five blocks to make a strip. Make six further strips of five blocks. Press the seams on half of the strips to one side, and on the other half to the other side. This will make the strips easier to join because the seam junctions will nestle together.

5 Join the strips together, pinning the seam junctions to prevent the seams from slipping and distorting the patchwork.

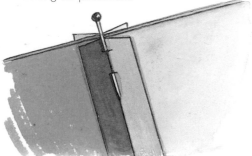

6 Stitch the shorter red border to the top edge and the shorter blue border to the bottom edge of the quilt with right sides together. Add the longer red border to the left-hand side of the quilt, and the longer blue border to the right-hand side.

7 Join the corners of the border in a mitred seam (see Finishing Corners, page 9) and press the completed quilt top.

8 Mark the border with the quilting pattern on page 42.

9 Lay the backing face down and put the wadding (batting) and pieced quilt on top to form a quilt sandwich. Use safety pins or tacking (basting) to hold the three layers together.

10 Quilt around the block design approx. 5mm (¼in) from the seams and along the border pattern.

11 Turn under 5mm (¼in) around the edges of both the backing and the quilt top. Quilt around this, approx. 32mm (⅛in) in from the edge.

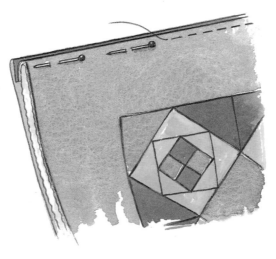

QUILTING PATTERN

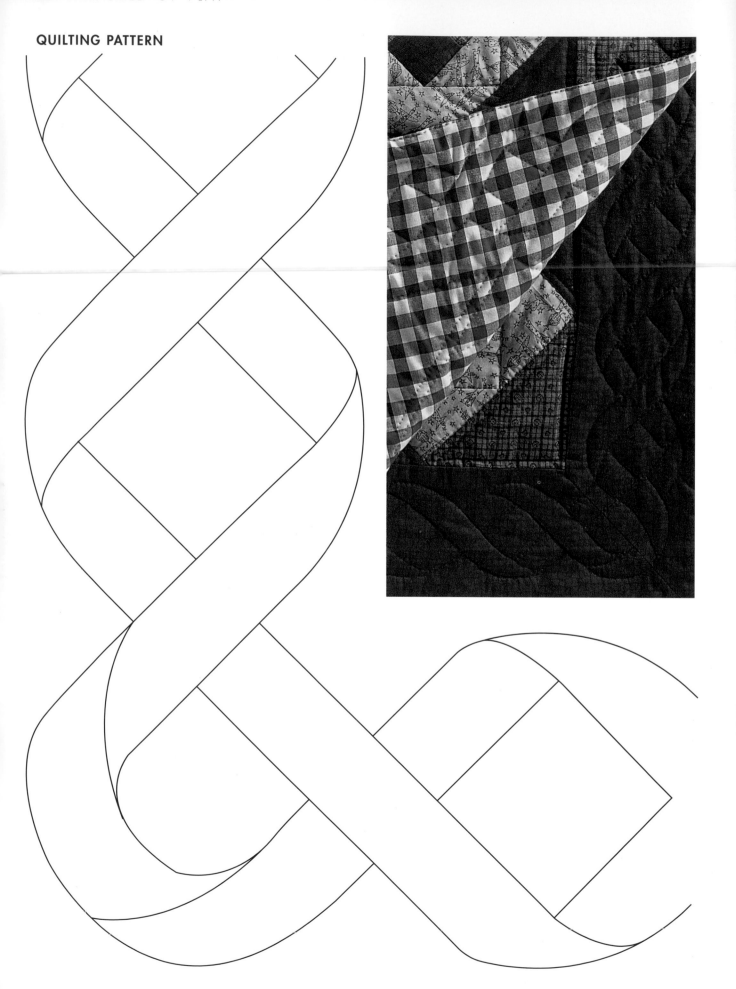

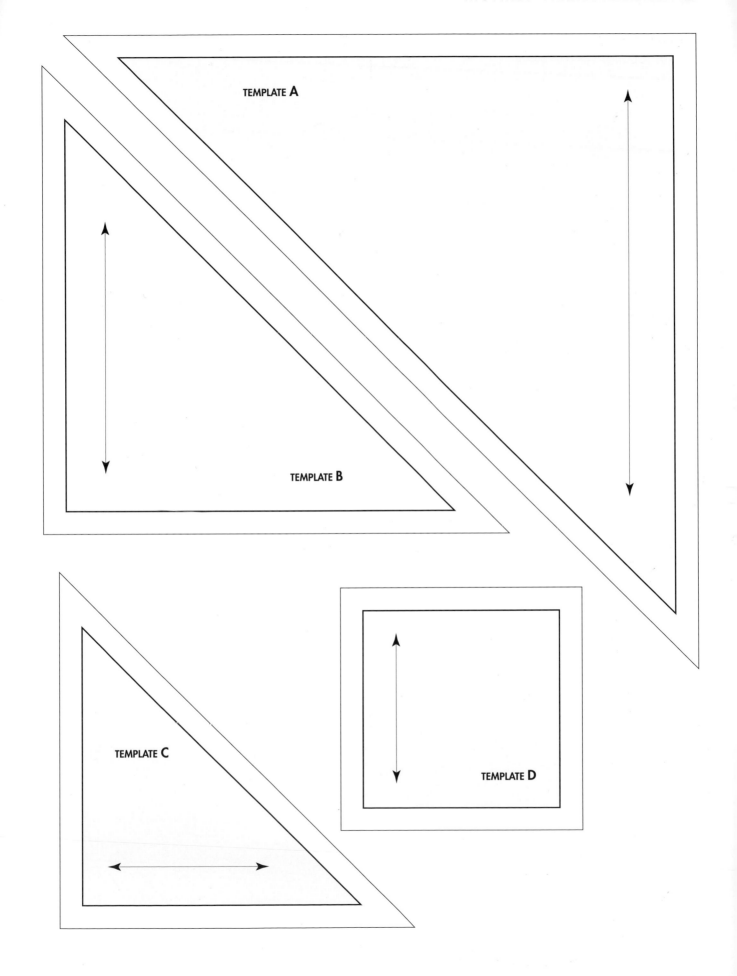

TEMPLATE A

TEMPLATE B

TEMPLATE C

TEMPLATE D

NOAH'S ARK FRIEZE

This very special project is designed for an adult to share with a child (see safety note). It tells the Bible story of Noah and the Ark through a panel of eight, colourful appliquéd squares. These can be hung as a frieze on a wall or folded and tied into a rag book. Although time-consuming, this panel is a pleasure to make – I enjoyed every minute.

YOU WILL NEED

◆ Selection of Kunin felt, (see suppliers page 127)
◆ Selection of plaid fabrics for backing the squares and for binding
◆ Buttons and beads (see safety note right)
◆ Sewing cotton
◆ Stranded embroidery cotton (floss)
◆ Strong cord, 1m (1yd)
◆ Greaseproof paper

TO MAKE THE BLOCKS

Note: The seam allowance throughout this project is 5mm (¼in). You will need to add it when cutting your appliqué pieces from fabric, but not when using felt. No seam allowance is shown on the templates for this reason.

1 First, make a template for the blocks. Cut a 22.8cm (9in) square of greaseproof paper and mark where the holes will go. Using a penny as a template, draw a circle 4.5cm (1¾in) from the top and another 4.5cm (1¾in) from the bottom, 1.27cm (½in) away from one edge of the template. This template will help you to make the hole positions on each block. Remember to check which side the holes should appear on each block, as they alternate throughout the frieze.

2 Make each block following the instructions on pages 46–61. When you are making an appliqué piece from fabric, tack (baste) around the piece as directed leaving the greaseproof

paper in place until you have nearly stitched all round the piece. Remove the tacking thread, then slip the paper out through the space you have left. Finish stitching the piece down.

TO MAKE THE FRIEZE

1 To assemble the frieze when all the blocks are complete, cut 32 strips of plaid fabrics 25.4cm (10in) long x 2.5cm (1in) wide.

2 Bind the top and bottom edges of block 1 (see Binding, page 9), then bind the left-hand edge, making sure that the ends are neatly turned in as you stitch.

3 Bind the top and bottom edges of the next block, then place the two blocks side by side. Stitch across the two blocks to join them together using a zig-zag stitch on your machine or by hand.

4 Pin and stitch a strip of plaid right sides together down the right side of the join.

5 Fold the ends of the plaid in, turn under the long edge, and fold it over the zig-zagging and hem stitch down.

6 Join all the other blocks in the correct order following steps 3–5. Finish off by binding the right edge of the last block. Remove any tacking (basting) stitches that are visible from the blocks.

TO MAKE INTO A BOOK

1 Cut the cord in half and knot all the ends.

2 Starting from the left side, fold the blocks back on themselves, and thread the cords through each set of holes.

3 Tie the cords into bows.

Kunin felt is stronger and easier to work than the usual felt you can buy, and is worth the extra cost for this project. When buying the plaid fabrics, look out for the small bundles of different fabrics you can buy from specialist quilting shops.

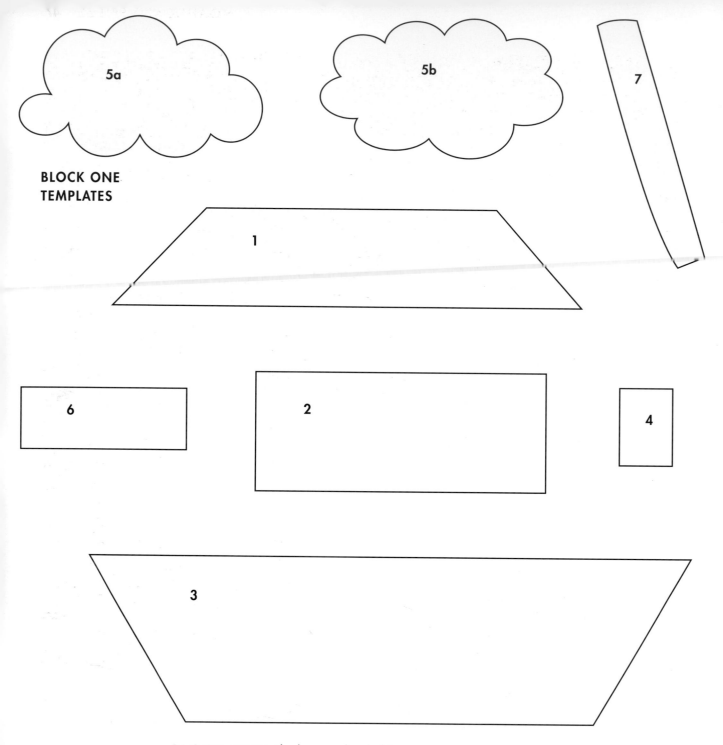

BLOCK ONE TEMPLATES

5a

5b

7

1

6

2

4

3

BLOCK ONE (holes to the left)

1 Cut a 22.8cm (9in) square of felt for the back of this block. This will give extra strength under the thinner sky fabric.

2 Cut a piece of green felt just over half the size of the block, and a piece of sky fabric to complete the square. Put the two pieces right sides together and hem stitch them together on the wrong side.

3 Trace Templates 1, 2 and 3 for the Ark onto greaseproof paper. Pin each piece to the wrong side of your chosen fabric. Fold the seam allowance to the wrong side and tack (baste) all round each piece. You only need to tack (baste) down the sides of Template 2.

4 Referring to the photograph, pin piece 2 in position on the background, followed by piece 1 and then piece 3. Hem stitch them all in place.

5 Using Template 4, cut a door from brown felt and blanket stitch in place on the Ark.

6 Using Template 5a and 5b, cut two clouds in grey felt and blanket stitch in place on the background.

7 Using Template 6, cut and tack (baste) three pieces of scaffold as described in step 3 and hem stitch to the background. Make and attach three planks using Template 7 in the same way.

8 Using the photograph above as your guide, quilt the lines on the Ark cabin 1cm (⅜in) apart using a darker thread.

9 I found Noah in a set of ceramic buttons I bought from the Bramble Patch (see Suppliers, page 127) and stitched him to the deck. If you cannot find this button, draw Noah with fabric pens and appliqué him in place, or leave him out altogether.

10 Tack (baste) the block to the backing fabric around all four sides.

11 Buttonhole stitch around both holes in a matching colour.

God decided he would punish the people for disobeying Him by destroying all life on Earth with a flood. He chose Noah to build an Ark to survive the flood. On the first page of your book you will see Noah building his Ark.

**BLOCK TWO
TEMPLATES**

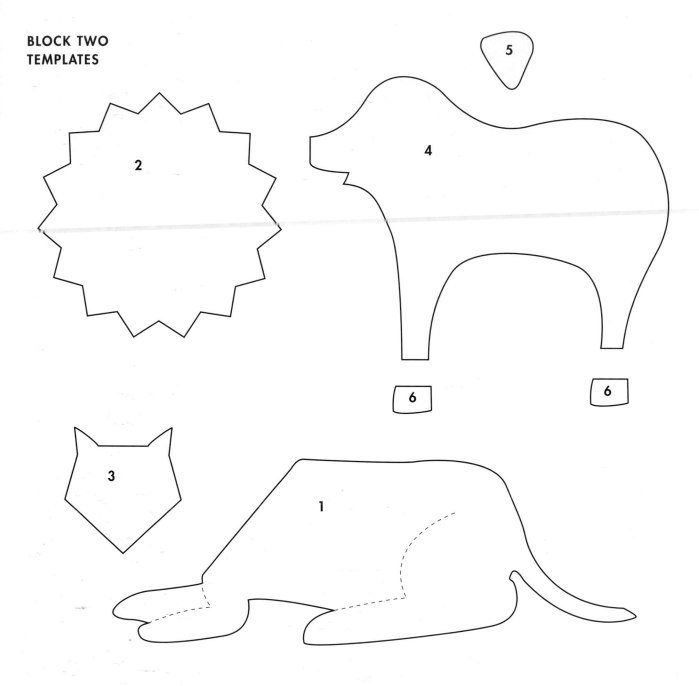

BLOCK TWO (holes to the right)

1 Cut two 22.8cm (9in) blocks, one in felt for the background and one in fabric for the backing. Mark the holes using the block template.

2 Using Template 1, cut the body of the lion from light brown felt.

3 Stitch the lion in place on the background using blanket stitch in a darker colour and marking in

his legs with stem stitch. Cut a fur tip for the lion's tail from a darker brown felt and stitch in place.

4 From Template 2, cut a mane in the darker brown felt. Pin this into place but do not stitch it down.

5 Cut the lion's face using Template 3. Pin and blanket stitch it in place over the mane. Embroider the lion's facial details as shown.

6 Trace Template 4 onto greaseproof paper. Pin this to the wrong side of your fabric. Fold the seam allowance to the wrong side and tack (baste) all round. Pin and hem stitch the pig to the background.

Cut the pig's ear and trotters from red felt using Templates 5 and 6 and slipstitch in place using a matching thread. Mark the mouth and tail with stem stitch in a darker colour. Sew on a bead for the eye.

7 Add animal buttons if desired.

8 Tack (baste) the block to the backing fabric around all four sides.

9 Buttonhole stitch around both holes in a matching colour.

Noah built his Ark strongly as God had told him. When it was finished, God asked Noah to take aboard a male and a female of all the animals and birds in the world.

**BLOCK THREE
TEMPLATES**

BLOCK 3 (holes to the left)

1 Cut two 22.8cm (9in) blocks, one in green felt for the background and one in fabric for the backing. Mark the holes using the block template.

2 Cut out the kangaroo from brown felt using Template 1, and appliqué in place on the background using blanket stitch. Outline the limbs in stem stitch. Cut out the joey's face using Template 2 and appliqué in place. Add the beads for its eyes.

3 Cut out the duck from white felt (Templates 3 and 4) and blanket stitch in position. Cut out two feet and a beak from yellow felt (Templates 5, 6 and 7), and attach in the same way. Sew on a bead eye. Add animal buttons if desired.

4 Tack (baste) the block to the backing fabric around all four sides.

5 Buttonhole stitch around both holes in a matching colour.

So Noah went out and found all the animals — from the mighty lion to the humble pig — and birds as God had asked and led them into his Ark.

**BLOCK FOUR
TEMPLATES**

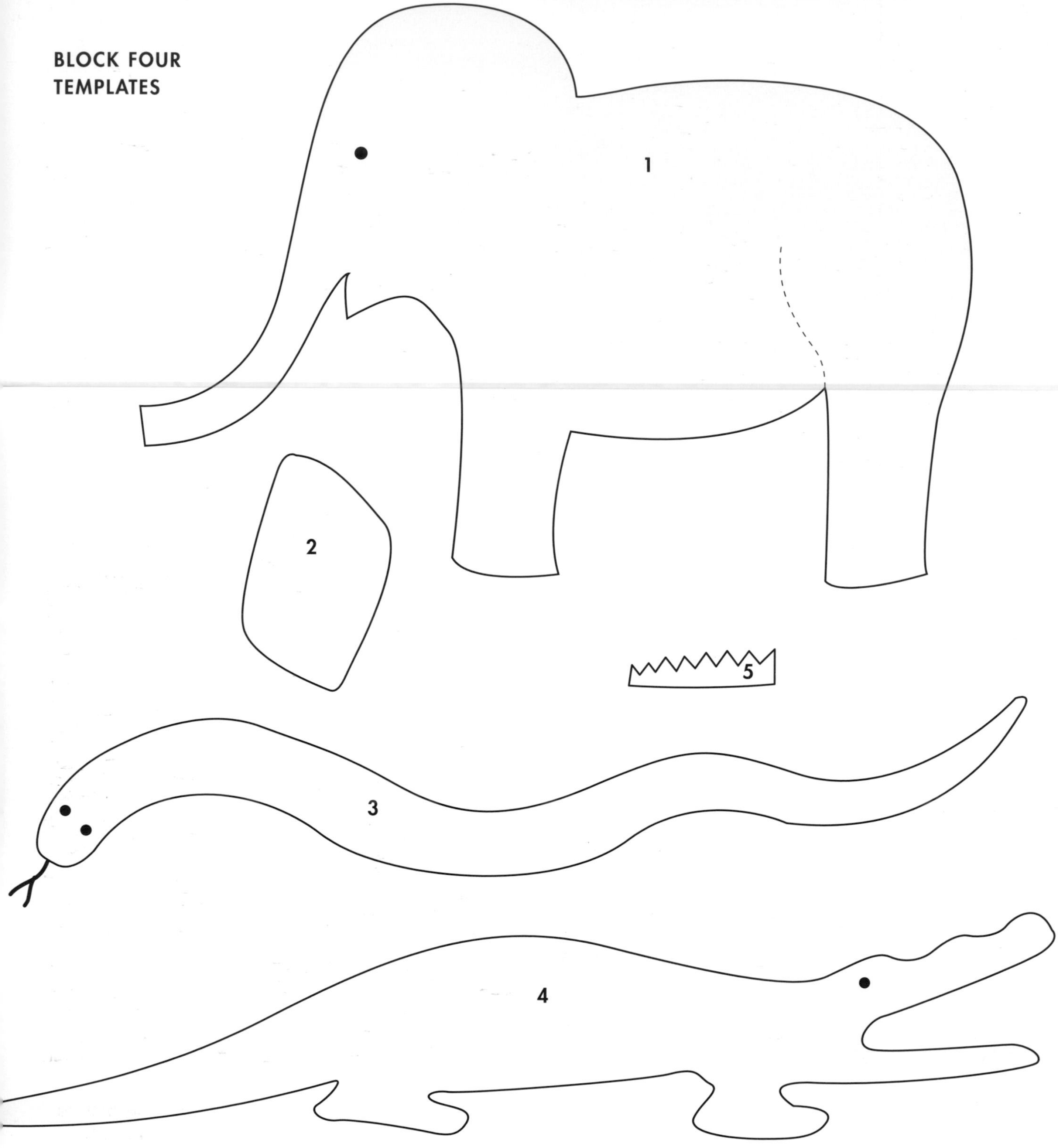

1

2

5

3

4

BLOCK FOUR (holes to the right)

1 Cut two 22.8cm (9in) blocks, one in brown felt for the background and one in fabric for the backing. Mark the holes using the block template.

2 Trace Template 1 onto greaseproof paper. Pin this to the wrong side of the fabric that you have chosen for the elephant. Fold the seam allowance to the wrong side and tack (baste) all round. Pin and hem stitch the elephant's body to the background. Cut two ear pieces using Template 2, one in the same fabric as the rest of the elephant and one in a contrasting fabric as a lining. Stitch them right sides together leaving a small opening

for turning. Turn through to the right side and hem stitch the opening closed. Hem stitch the ear in place on the elephant and sew on the bead for its eye.

3 Appliqué the snake in place on the background following step 2 and using Template 3. Add the beads for its eyes and embroider the forked tongue as shown in the photograph.

4 Appliqué the crocodile in place following

step 2 and using Template 4. Cut two strips of felt using Template 5 for its teeth and sew them in place while you are attaching the crocodile body. Add the bead for its eye. Add animal buttons if desired.

5 Tack (baste) the block to the backing fabric around all four sides.

6 Buttonhole stitch around both holes in a matching colour.

The animals are made from appliquéd felt and fabric. Additional ceramic or wooden animal buttons can be added for extra interest. Children will enjoy picking out all the different ones they can see.

BLOCK FIVE
TEMPLATES

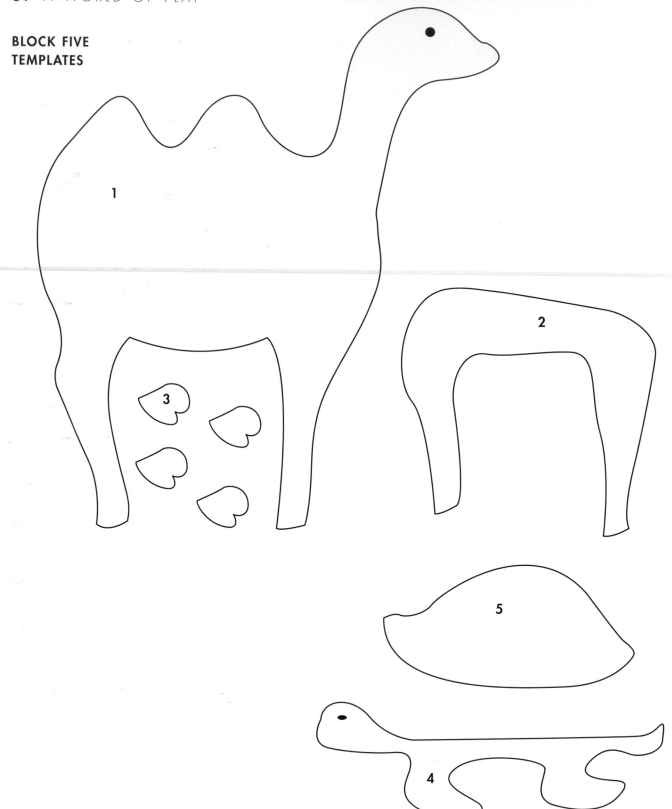

BLOCK FIVE (holes to the left)

1 Cut two 22.8cm (9in) blocks, one in green felt for the background and one in fabric for the backing. Mark the holes using the block template.

2 Trace Templates 1 and 2 onto greaseproof

paper. Pin these to the wrong side of your chosen fabrics for the camel. Fold the seam allowance to the wrong side and tack (baste) all round. Hem stitch piece 2 (the camel's far legs) to the background first and then hem stitch the main camel piece after. Cut a small piece of felt for the ear,

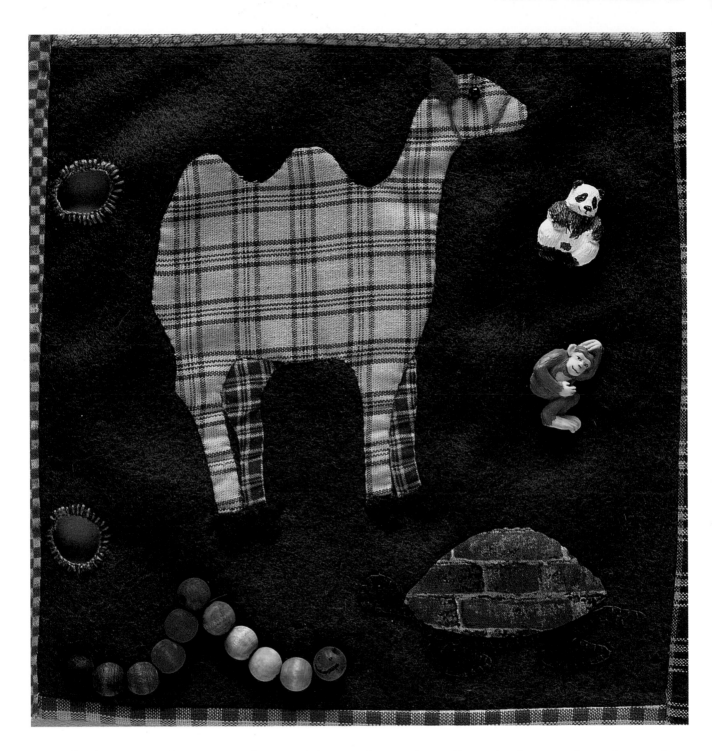

and the four feet using Template 3. Hem stitch them all in place. Add the bead for the eye. Referring to the photograph embroider the tail and bridle detail in stem stitch.

3 Cut the body and head of the tortoise from brown felt using Template 4 and blanket stitch in position. Trace the shell on to your chosen fabric using Template 5 and tack (baste) down following step 2. Hem stitch this on top of the felt body. Sew the bead eye in position.

4 The caterpillar was designed by my daughter Briony and is made up of wooden beads painted with felt pens that were then stitched in place. The antennae were embroidered afterwards. Add animal buttons if desired.

5 Tack (baste) the block to the backing fabric around all four sides.

6 Buttonhole stitch around both holes in a matching colour.

From tortoises to camels, and tiny caterpillars and lizards, every species could be found inside Noah's Ark when it was loaded.

BLOCK SIX
TEMPLATES

(templates labelled 1–9 as illustrated)

BLOCK SIX (holes to the right)

1 Cut two 22.8cm (9in) blocks, one in felt for the background and one in fabric for the backing. Mark the holes using the block template.

2 Cut out the sheep's body from white felt using Template 1 and appliqué in place on the background using blanket stitch. Cut the face and legs from black felt using Templates 2 and 3 and attach in the same way. Sew on the bead eyes.

3 Cut the snail's body from pale brown felt using Template 4 and appliqué in place as before. Trace the shell (Template 5) onto greaseproof paper and pin this to the wrong side of your fabric. Tack (baste) down the seam allowance and hem stitch the shell in place on the snail. Mark the shell contours in stem stitch. Embroider the antennae and add a French knot at the tip of each one. Sew on the bead eyes and embroider the face.

4 Cut out the pieces for the lizard using Templates 6–9 and pin in place (you may find it helpful to hold the edges together with a dab of glue). Zig-zag across the joins and blanket stitch the lizard to the background. Sew on the beads for the eyes.

5 I sewed a lovely tiger button over some felt leaves to make it look as if its head is appearing through them. Add other animal buttons if desired.

6 Tack (baste) the block to the backing fabric around all four sides.

7 Buttonhole stitch around both holes in a matching colour.

Then God made it rain for 40 days and 40 nights. The Earth was covered with water that rose higher than the tallest mountains. Every living thing was swept away except for Noah and his family and all the animals in the Ark.

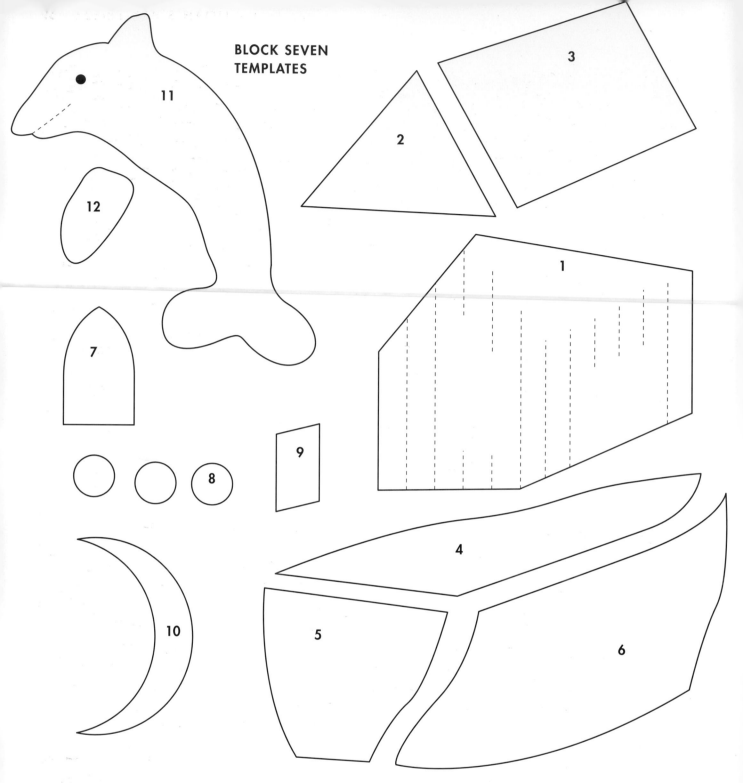

BLOCK SEVEN TEMPLATES

BLOCK SEVEN (holes to the left)

1 Cut a 22.8cm (9in) block in felt for the backing, a piece of blue felt approx. two thirds of the block depth, and fabric printed with stars for the sky approx. half of the block depth. Cut waves along the top of the felt, place it over the star-print fabric, and blanket stitch the fabrics in white along this curved edge.

2 Trace the pieces for the Ark on to greaseproof paper using Templates 1–6 and pin these to the back of your fabrics. Tack (baste) down the seam allowance on each one.

3 Appliqué the Ark to the background using hem stitch in the following order: first, attach the back of the roof (2), sew the back of the hull (4) into place, then hem stitch the Ark cabin (1) over it and put the roof front (3) on top. Sew the hull together (5 and 6) and lay it over the cabin. Hem

stitch in place. Using the photograph as a guide, cut a wavy line in the felt and push the bottom of the Ark under it. Blanket stitch in white along this new wave, anchoring the Ark as you go. Hem stitch the rest of the hull in place.

4 Cut a window, a door and three portholes from gold felt using Templates 7, 8 and 9, and blanket stitch in place (see photograph for placement).

5 Blanket stitch another two waves beneath and below the Ark as shown in the photograph.

6 Cut the moon from yellow felt (Template 10) and the dolphin from grey felt (Template 11) and appliqué in place with blanket stitches. Appliqué a fin to the dolphin using Template 12 and sew on a bead eye. Add star and animal buttons if desired.

7 Tack (baste) the block to the backing fabric around all four sides.

8 Buttonhole stitch around both holes in a matching colour.

For 150 days and nights the Ark floated on the water, and here you can see it floating at night under the stars. They do have some friends, however – you can see them in the water.

**BLOCK EIGHT
TEMPLATES**

BLOCK EIGHT (holes to the right)

1 Cut a 22.8cm (9in) block in felt for the backing and a piece of blue felt, half block depth, for the sea and blue fabric, two-thirds block depth, for the sky. Mark the holes using the block template.

2 Trace the island onto greaseproof paper using Template 1, cut from your chosen fabric and tack (baste) down the seam allowance. Cut the whale from grey felt using Template 2. Appliqué these pieces in place on the sky fabric using hem stitch for the island and blanket stitch for the whale.

3 Cut a wavy edge to the sea fabric. Place the sea fabric at the bottom edge of the island and blanket stitch in place.

4 Appliqué the Ark into place using Templates 3, 4 and 5; add a door cut from brown felt using Template 6. Quilt the lines on the Ark cabin as shown in the photograph.

5 Embroider the whale's mouth in stem stitch. Add a bead eye and stitch a running stitch spray referring to the photograph.

6 Cut the trunk and frond of the palm tree from felt using Templates 7 and 8. Appliqué the trunk with blanket stitch and put the frond on top, then stitch three black beads for coconuts through the frond to hold it in place.

7 Add buttons as desired. If you do not have a dove button, draw a dove with fabric pens and appliqué it in place.

8 Tack (baste) the block to the backing fabric around all four sides.

9 Buttonhole stitch around both holes in a matching colour

Noah sent out a dove out to find land. When it returned with a branch in its mouth, Noah knew land was near. On the last page you can see the Ark as it reaches dry land at last. The dove is sitting on the roof.

Moving
On

The Old Maid's Puzzle quilt is an ideal design to choose if you want to make a quilt for a child that will last for many years. Store a special badge collection on the Pastel Badge wall hanging or choose the Initial wall hanging to celebrate a child's name. Who can resist the marvellous Felicity's Friends? Every little girl would love this quilt.

6–9 years

OLD MAID'S PUZZLE QUILT

A child will treasure this quilt for many years. The traditional design lends itself beautifully to the soft colours used here, and it would work well in primary colours, too. It is a straightforward block to make that can be set in various ways to build up an interesting design. Look carefully at the quilt and you will see the stars that are formed when four blocks are joined together. You can vary your colours to enhance these stars.

FINISHED SIZE 223.5cm x 183cm (88 x 72in)
BLOCK SIZE 41cm (16in)

YOU WILL NEED

◆ Mid-blue fabric, 1m (1yd) x 112cm (44in) wide
◆ Mid-pink fabric, 50cm (½yd) by 112cm (44in) wide
◆ Mid-green and lilac gingham, 25cm (¼yd) by 112cm (44in) wide of each
◆ Pale-pink patterned fabric for background, 2m (2¼yds) by 112cm (44in) wide
◆ Pale pink fabric, 4m (4.5yds) by 112cm (44in) wide
◆ Blue patterned fabric, 1m (1yd) by 112cm (44in) wide for borders
◆ Pink bias binding, 9m (9yds)
◆ Wadding, 229 x 188cm (90 x 74in) piece
◆ Matching quilting thread

A 5mm (¼in) seam allowance is used throughout

1 Wash and press the fabrics.

2 From the blue patterned fabric make two strips 11.5 x 226cm (4½ x 89in) and two strips 11.5 x 165cm (4½ x 65in) for borders. You will have to join the strips to make the required lengths.

3 Trace off and make Templates 1–3 on page 67 (see Seam Allowance Rule, page 7). Cut out the following pieces (see Rotary Cutting, page 7):
   40 x Template 3 in mid-blue fabric
   34 x Template 2 in mid-green fabric
   62 x Template 2 in mid-pink fabric
   200 x Template 2 in pale pink patterned fabric
   28 x Template 2 in lilac gingham fabric
   80 x Template 1 in pale pink patterned fabric

4 Make the first block following the exploded block piecing diagram right. Assemble the pieces following the numbered order and using a 5mm (¼in) seam allowance throughout. Using the quilt piecing diagram on page 66 as a guide to placing the colours, make 19 more blocks in this way.

5 Sew the blocks together in rows following the quilt piecing diagram on page 66.

6 Press the completed quilt top. Add the two longer border strips to the sides of the quilt with right sides together and using a 5mm (¼in) seam allowance. Add the shorter strips to the top and bottom in the same way. Press once again.

EXPLODED BLOCK PIECING DIAGRAM

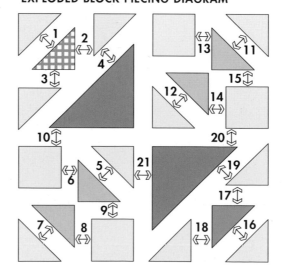

7 Transfer the cable quilting pattern, page 67, on to the border and mark a heart in the centre of each square using the heart template on page 75 and the photograph as a guide.

8 Lay the backing face down and put the wadding (batting) and pieced quilt on top to form a quilt sandwich. Use safety pins or tacking (basting) to hold the three layers together.

9 Quilt around all the marked lines and outline quilt each block, about 5mm (¼in) away from the seams.

10 Bind the quilt with the bias binding (see Binding, page 9).

Use four blocks of this pattern to make a matching cushion cover. Choose fabric colours that will highlight the star motif and add the border if desired

QUILT PIECING DIAGRAM

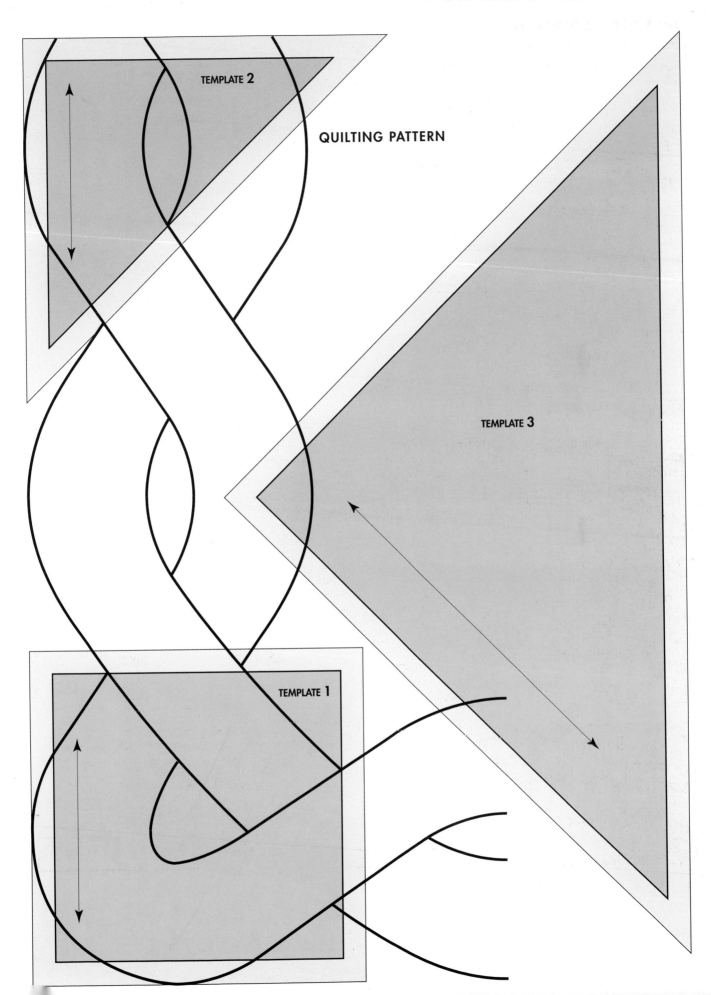

TEMPLATE 2

QUILTING PATTERN

TEMPLATE 3

TEMPLATE 1

PASTEL BADGE WALL HANGING

Children love collecting badges whether they're the decorative ones bought on a special day out, achievement or merit badges they have earned, or one from the front of a birthday card. However, as anyone with such a collection will tell you, it's difficult to find a good way of displaying your badges, and they usually end up in an old biscuit tin. This wall hanging will help. Both practical and attractive to look at, the crosshatch quilting provides perfect spaces for pinning precious badges.

1 Wash and press the fabrics.

2 Trace off and make Templates A, B and C on page 71 (see Seam Allowance Rule, page 7).

3 Following the quilting/piecing diagram on page 71 as a colour reference, use the templates to cut enough pieces from the scrap fabrics to make four Flying Star blocks and four Card Trick blocks (see page 70). Join the pieces following the numbered order shown on the exploded block diagrams and using a 5mm (¼in) seam allowance throughout.

4 Cut eight 11.5cm (4½in) squares in blue fabric and one 31.75cm (12½in) square in blue fabric.

Cut one 51cm (21in) square for the backing.

5 Using the quilting/piecing diagram on page 71 as a guide, make two strips containing one patchwork and two plain squares and stitch them to each side of the centre square. Piece three patchwork and two plain blocks together to form a strip. Sew this to the centre square panel. Make another strip in the same way and sew this to the bottom of the centre square. Press the completed top.

6 Mark the quilt top with lines for the crosshatch quilting following the quilting/piecing diagram.

7 Lay the backing, wadding (batting) and pieced top together to form a quilt sandwich. Use safety pins or tacking (basting) to hold the three layers together.

8 Quilt the crosshatch design starting in the middle and working outwards. Outline quilt the patchwork blocks 5mm (¼in) away from the seams.

9 Bind the hanging with 51 x 2.5cm (21 x 1in) strips made from scrap fabrics.

FINISHED SIZE
51 x 51cm (20 x 20in)

YOU WILL NEED
- Scraps of fabrics for the patchwork blocks and binding
- Pale blue chambray fabric, 75cm (¾yd) for the front and back
- Thin, low-loft wadding (batting), 51 x 51cm (21 x 21in)
- Matching quilting thread
- One wooden net rod or pole for hanging

A 5mm (¼in) seam allowance is used throughout

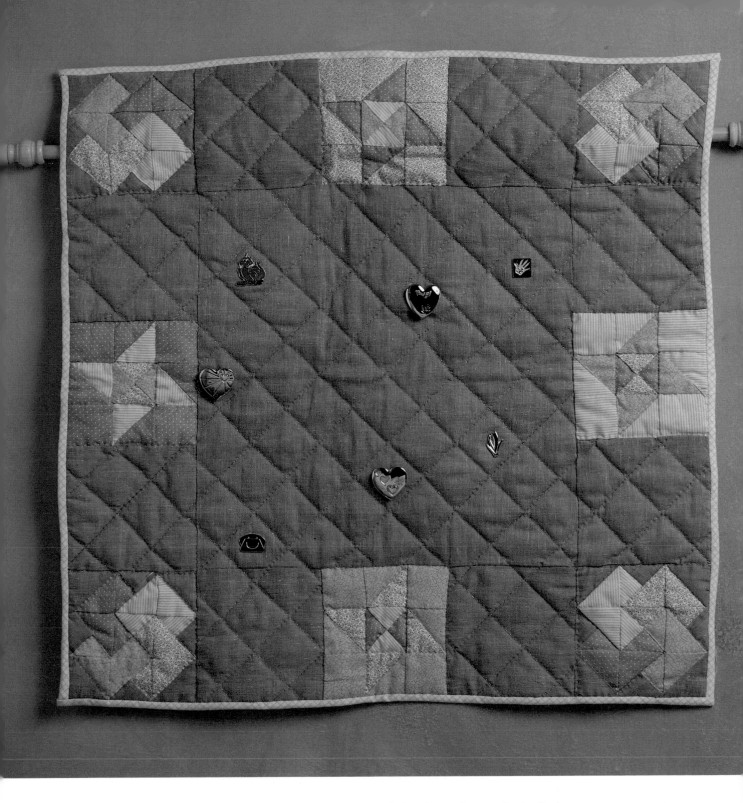

10 Cut a strip of chambray fabric 10cm (4in) shorter than the width of your wall hanging to make a sleeve for the pole or rod on the back. Hem both short edges.

11 Fold the fabric in half lengthways with right sides together and join the raw edges in a 5mm (¼in) seam to make a tube. Turn this to the right side and press, keeping the seam in the centre.

12 Hem stitch the tube in place on the back of your wall hanging about 5cm (2in) down from the top edge. Try not to let your stitches show through on the front.

13 Thread a pole or rod through the sleeve. This will hold the top edge firm and take the strain off the quilt.

CARD TRICK EXPLODED BLOCK PIECING DIAGRAM

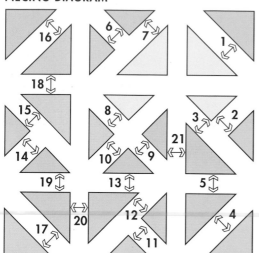

FLYING STAR EXPLODED BLOCK PIECING DIAGRAM

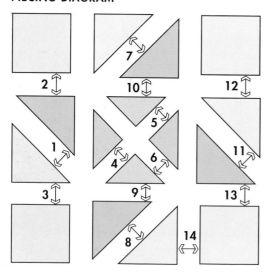

Use two of these small 10cm (4in) square blocks to make a purse for a child. Join three edges together using a .25cm (¼in) seam allowance and insert a zip in the top edge.

QUILTING/PIECING DIAGRAM

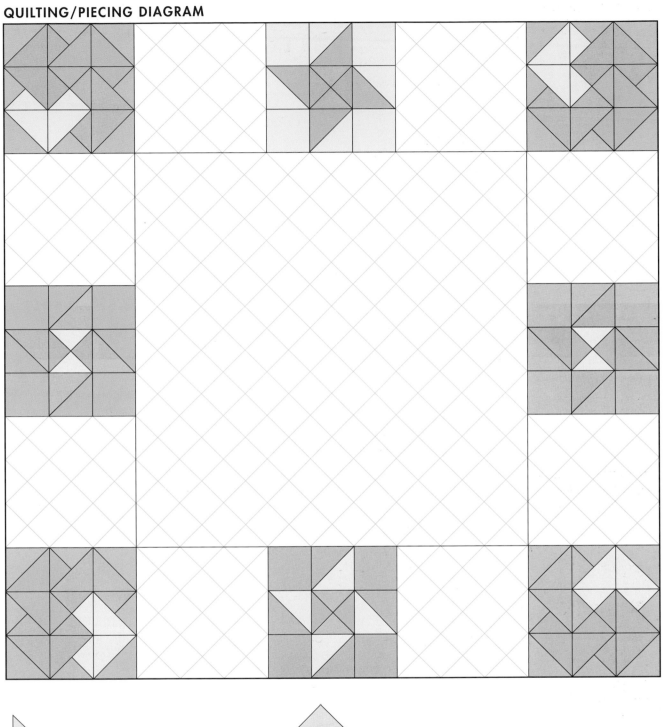

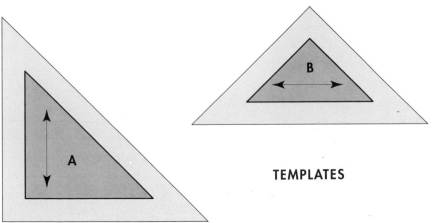

TEMPLATES

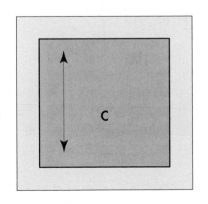

INITIAL HEART WALL HANGING

Here's a delightful way to brighten up a child's bedroom wall: an appliqué heart wall hanging spelling out the child's initial. It's an ideal way to use up leftover scraps of fabric and is very simple to make. It would also be an excellent way to try out some of the more fancy stitches on a new sewing machine. Why not make several and spell out a name?

1 Press the background and backing fabrics. Lay the backing fabric to one side.

2 Using a ruler and sharp pencil, mark a grid on the background fabric. You need seven rows of seven 7cm (2¾in) squares.

3 Pin or tack (baste) the background fabric, wadding (batting) and backing fabric together. Sew along the marked grid lines using decorative sewing machine stitches. Alternatively, embroider by hand in feather stitch.

4 Trace off the heart template on page 75 and cut out from card. Use this template to mark 49 hearts on one side of the thin plain fabric, leaving a gap of at least 1.5cm (½in) inbetween.

5 Referring to the alphabet on pages 73–75, cut out the number of hearts you need for your initial as a strip. Place this right sides together with the initial heart fabric and pin the centre of each heart. Machine stitch around the outline of each heart leaving no opening for turning. Repeat this with the fabric for the base hearts.

6 When you have stitched all the hearts, cut them out carefully leaving a small seam allowance (approx. 25mm/⅛in) around each one.

7 Make a small slit in the plain fabric on the back of each heart. Turn the heart to the right side through this slit. Use the point of a knitting needle to smooth the seam through the slit. Press the completed hearts so that the edges are sharp.

8 Lay the prepared grid flat, place all the hearts on the right squares following the alphabet on pages 73–75 and pin in place. You will find it helpful to tack (baste) them down with a couple of stitches and remove the pins. Sew each heart into place using invisible hemming.

9 Bind your hanging with the bias binding (see Binding, page 9).

10 Add a sleeve to the back of your wall hanging following the instructions given for the Pastel Badge wall hanging, page 68) and thread a rod or pole through it.

FINISHED SIZE 50 x 50cm (20 x 20in)

YOU WILL NEED
- Fabric for the background, 55cm (22in) square (I used a hand-dyed multi-coloured piece)
- White fabric for backing, 50cm (½ yd) by 112cm (44in) wide
- Fabric for the base hearts, 50cm (½yd) by 112cm (44in) wide
- Fabric for the initial hearts, 25cm (¼yd) by 112cm (44in) wide
- Thin plain fabric (old sheeting can be used), 75cm (¾yd) by 112cm (44in)
- Cotton wadding, 55cm (22in) square
- Matching thread for machine or hand embroidery
- Matching bias binding, 1.25m (1¼yds) by 2.5cm (1in) wide
- One wooden net rod or pole for hanging

A 5mm (¼in) seam allowance is used throughout

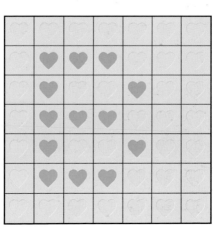

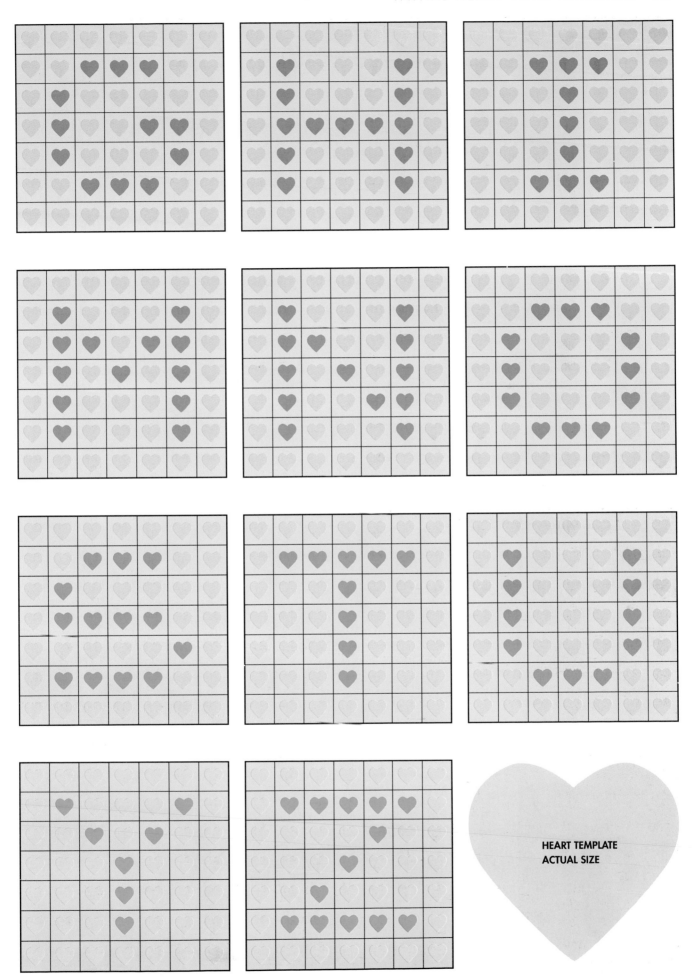

**HEART TEMPLATE
ACTUAL SIZE**

FELICITY'S FRIENDS

I took the idea for this special quilt I made for my niece Felicity from a traditional patchwork block called Paperdoll. I adapted the design to give each doll legs, shoes and hands. However, this meant that the dolls could not be placed side by side on the quilt because their hands got in the way. To get round this I offset each row of dolls and added a kite, some balloons and a lace butterfly at the top. At the bottom I made little stuffed legs for Laura and Catherine that hang down over the border.

FINISHED SIZE
183 x 143cm (72 x 56in)

YOU WILL NEED
- Blue fabric, 1.5m (1¾yds) by 112 (44in) wide for background
- Pink fabric, 75cm (¾yd) by 112 (44in) wide for hands, legs and faces
- Pink patterned fabric, 3m (3yds) by 112 (44in) wide for borders and backing
- Assorted fabrics for dolls' clothes
- Buttons, beads, lace and ribbon for embellishing the outfits
- Matching thread
- Blue quilting thread
- Blue bias binding, 7.5m (7½yds) by 2.5cm (1in) wide

A 5mm (¼in) seam allowance is used throughout

TO MAKE THE BLOCKS

1 Wash and press the fabrics. Trace off and make Templates 1–10 on pages 80–81 (see Seam Allowance Rule, page 7). Cut out the following pieces:

    16 x Template 1 in pink for the faces
    28 x Template 8 in pink for the legs
    70 x Template 3 in blue for the background
    32 x Template 5 in blue for the background
    32 x Template 6 in blue for the background
    14 x Template 7 in blue for the background
    54 x Template 2 in blue for the background
    30 x Template 10 in pink for the hands

For each doll cut 1 x Template 3 on the fold, 2 x Template 4 and 2 x Template 6 in your chosen dress fabric. For each doll, excluding Laura and Catherine, cut 2 x Template 9 in your chosen shoe fabric.

2 Keep the pieces for each doll separate in an envelope or plastic bag, and make them one by one. Join the pieces following the numbered order in the exploded block piecing diagram and using a 5mm (¼in) seam throughout. Insert the lace trimming between the pieces at this stage where required. Tack (baste) the hands to the ends of the sleeves. They will be attached when the dolls are pieced together at the end.

3 Mark the features on the face using Template 1 and embroider these in stem stitch. Sew on buttons for the eyes. Press your pieced doll and add the details to each one (see pages 78–79).

TEMPLATE KEY

EXPLODED BLOCK PIECING DIAGRAM

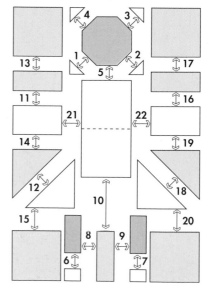

1 RUBY

Add Ruby's hair using dark brown perlé cotton. Pull the thread through the fabric leaving about 3.8cm (1½in) on the front. Take a backstitch, and bring the thread back out. Cut it to leave a 3.8cm (1½in) end. Work further stitches in this way around the hairline. Sew a line of crystal beads around the neckline and wrist for Ruby's bracelet and necklace. Quilt a small heart on her chest.

2 LORNA

Dressed in her Sunday best, we can see only the back view of Lorna as she is shown walking away. Cut a 15cm (6in) circle from cardboard and use it to mark the hat fabric. Cut out leaving a 5mm (¼in) seam allowance. Cut a circle of wadding, the same size as the hat. Place the wadding and the card in the centre on the wrong side of the fabric. Tack (baste) around the circle and gather the fabric around the wadding and cardboard. Fasten off securely, and ease the cardboard out of the circle. Make a 8cm (3in) cardboard circle and repeat the process for the crown of the hat. Make a ribbon bow, leave fairly long ends, and sew to the bottom of the crown. Hem stitch the finished hat in place on the doll.

3 CHARLOTTE

Charlotte has three sheep buttons on her dress because she is a farmer's daughter. Piece the doll as usual, but use two Template 2 pieces in white fabric for her mop-cap and trim with lace. Put lace at the bottom of her skirt too, and sew it between the skirt edge and leg pieces. Securely sew the three sheep buttons down the front of the dress.

4 OLIVIA

Sew Olivia's hair in the same way as Ruby's but make each length of thread 20cm (8in). Part the hair in the middle and tie in two bunches with ribbon bows. Add a lace pocket and hem stitch a 'V' of lace as shown before piecing the doll.

5 STEPHANIE

Add a small lace-topped pocket with a teddy bear button peeping out of it to Stephanie's dress. Sew her hair in the same way as Ruby's using yellow thread and cutting the ends short. Make the kite using the template on page 83 and tack (baste) around the edges ready to appliqué it in position. Leave this until you assemble the quilt top.

6 KIMBERLEY

Piece the doll as usual, but use two Template 2 pieces in pink for her hat and trim with lace. Attach ribbon roses and scraps of ribbon to each side of her head. Trim the edge of her dress with lace and make her bridesmaid's bouquet from several ribbon roses stitched together with two lengths of ribbon. Stitch the bouquet to the centre of her left hand.

7 FIONA

Cut a 11.5 x 13cm (4½ x 5in) piece of white fabric for Fiona's nurse's cap. Fold up one third of the fabric, then fold down the remaining third of the fabric over it. Tack along the raw edge and fold the brim back. Pin this to the headpiece, leaving room for the eyes, and piece the first row of the block as usual. Cut a 10 x 13cm (4 x 5in) piece of white fabric for the apron and turn under a 5mm (¼in) hem. Cut four 2.5cm (1in) squares in white and turn under a 5mm (¼in) hem on two sides of each. Using the photograph as a guide, hem stitch the straps to the apron and the apron in place on the dress. Piece the rest of the block as usual. Draw a red cross with a fabric crayon on the hat and the apron. Draw a fob watch on the apron with a permanent black felt pen.

8 LAURA

Make the bandage on Laura's head following the instructions for Fiona's hat. Fold the brim so that it is crooked to create the effect of a bandage. First cut four 10 x 5cm (4 x 3in) pieces of flesh fabric and four 10 x 3.8cm (4 x 1¾in) strips of fabric for the shoes. Sew a shoe piece to each leg piece and press the seams. Place two pieces right sides together. Using the leg template on page 83, draw out the leg shape on to the fabric. Cut out leaving a 5mm (¼in) seam allowance. Sew around the drawn line, then turn to the right side. Repeat. Stuff both legs lightly, leaving at least 5mm (¼in) free at the top for attaching to the quilt, then put the legs to one side. Attach these to the quilt with the border. Mark a heart on Laura's chest to be quilted later. Laura's mouth turns down rather than up.

9 LUCY

Trim the dress with lace at the neck and hemline. Sew Lucy's hair in the same way as Ruby's, cutting the threads long enough to tie in bunches. Then add a fringe in the same way, this time cutting the threads shorter. Add the balloons when assembling the quilt top.

10 CARLY

Piece the doll as usual, but use two Template 2 pieces in brown fabric for her hair and enclose two plaits in the seam. You can knot her hair as on the other dolls instead if you prefer, leaving long strands to plait. Tie ribbon bows on the plaits. Carly has a lace-edged yoke on her dress. Draw a semi-circle on the back of a piece of contrasting fabric. Cut out, leaving a 5mm (¼in) seam allowance. Turn a 5mm (¼in) hem to the wrong side and add lace. Appliqué this to the chest of the doll before piecing in the usual way.

11 VERITY

Piece the doll as usual adding lace to the top of her shoes and along the neck of her dress. The hair is blonde – make this as before leaving the ends long, parting them at one side and tying them into bunches. Make a small drawstring bag and fill it with a few items. Sew a half press-stud to the palm of Verity's left hand, and the other half to the back of the bag for attaching it to the doll.

12 BRIONY

Plait a long length of brown thread for Briony's hair long enough to stretch from one shoulder to the other. Tie the ends carefully and add ribbon bows. Hem stitch in place. Attach another ribbon bow to the top of her head. Piece the doll in the usual way adding a lace trim to the hem of her dress. Cut two 15cm (6in) squares of fabric for Briony's satchel and sew them together with right sides facing, in a 5mm (¼in) seam, leaving a 2.5cm (1in) opening for turning. Turn to the right side and push the corners straight with the point of a knitting needle. Slipstitch the opening together. Fold the square into an envelope, and slip-stitch the sides together leaving the flap open. Hem stitch the satchel at an angle to Briony's skirt. Sew a half press-stud under the top flap, and the other half to the satchel. Stitch a heart button on the top flap, and buttons in the shape of a pencil sharpener, ruler and pencil inside. Sew a thin ribbon strap from the left shoulder to the satchel, and around her waist as shown.

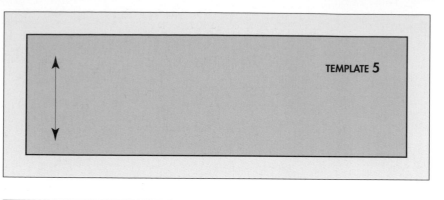

TEMPLATE 5

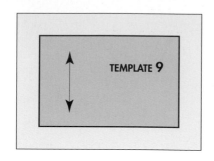

TEMPLATE 9

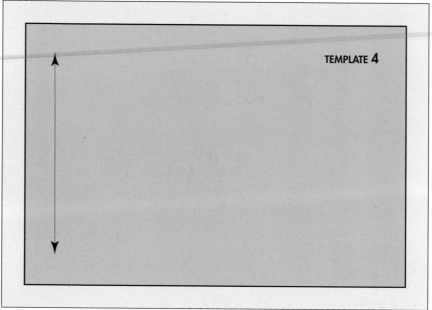

TEMPLATE 4

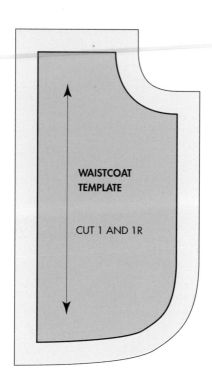

WAISTCOAT
TEMPLATE

CUT 1 AND 1R

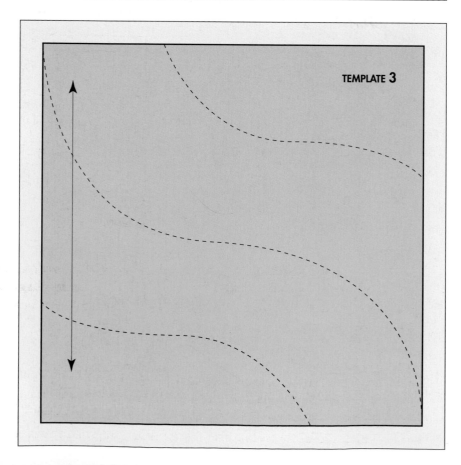

TEMPLATE 3

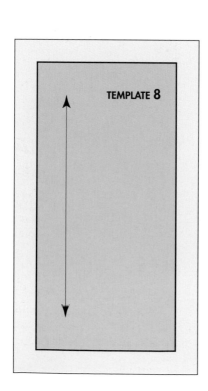

TEMPLATE 8

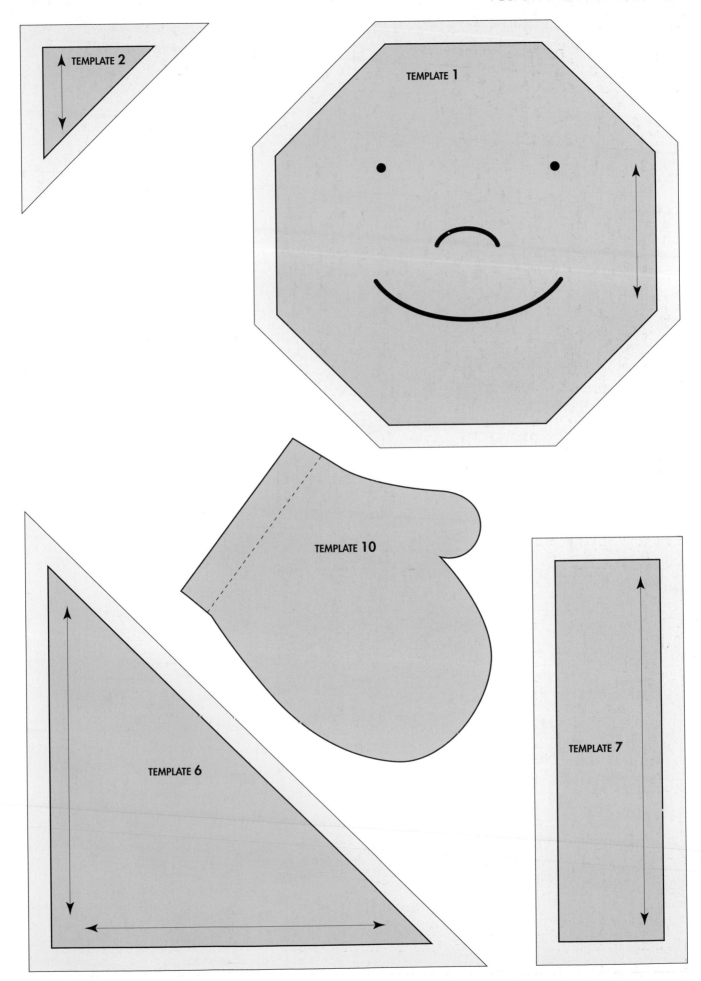

TEMPLATE 2

TEMPLATE 1

TEMPLATE 10

TEMPLATE 6

TEMPLATE 7

13 KATY

Piece the doll as usual, but use two Template 2 pieces in pink for her hat and trim with lace. Make her shoes to match. Add freckles to her nose when you mark the face. Hem stitch some pink ribbon for a belt with a bra strap adjuster as a buckle. She has two other accessories – a jewel pendant and a little bag. Fasten this to her hand by a length of ribbon with half a press-stud at each end. Sew the ribbon firmly to her right hand.

14 LISA

Lisa is dressed for cold weather. Her hat is made in the same way as Fiona's nurse's cap, but pieced along the hairline as in the photograph. She is wearing gloves so make her hands in the same fabric as the hat and scarf. Cut a 15 x 5cm (6 x 2in) strip of fabric for her scarf. Fold in half lengthways with right sides together and join the long edges in a 5mm (¼in) seam. Turn to the right side and hem stitch the ends together. Knot threads at one end to form a fringe. Piece the doll as usual adding lace to the hem of her dress, then hem stitch the scarf to the neckline, fold it down at the right edge and hem stitch down. Embroider a large star at the top of the hat as a bobble and sew a snowman button to the dress.

15 LAURA JANE

Like Lorna this doll is also shown walking away and has a long plait and a bow on the back of her dress. Cut two 30.5 x 5cm (12 x 2in) strips in the dress fabric and turn under a 5mm (¼in) hem down both sides and one end of each piece. Pin the raw edges to either side of the waist on the dress, taking two or three tucks in the bow piece. Make the doll as usual, then tie the bow. Make the hair by knotting long strands all around the hairline. Plait the hair into one plait, and tie a pink bow to the end.

16 CATHERINE

Piece the doll as usual, but use two Template 2 pieces in purple fabric for her hat and trim with lace. Cut two waistcoat pieces, using the waistcoat template on page 80, remembering to make one reversed. Turn under a 5mm (¼in) hem on all edges and hem stitch this in place on the dress. Blanket stitch around the front opening. Add a small pendant if desired. Make the legs in the same way as Laura's and attach these at the same time as the border.

To prevent the hands flapping around, make a small invisible stitch under each one.

TO ASSEMBLE THE QUILT

1 Cut two 153 x 11.5cm (60 x 4½in) strips and two 193 x 11.5cm (76 x 4½in) strips in pink for the borders. You may need to join two strips to make the right length.

2 Join all the pieced dolls together in vertical strips using the photograph as a guide. You will need to add a strip of three blue background squares using Template 3 above Stephanie and Katy's heads. Make a small invisible stitch under each hand to prevent it from flapping around.

3 Place Laura and Catherine's legs in position on the edge of the dress and tack (baste) these right sides together. Sew the longer border pieces to the sides of the quilt using a 5mm (¼in) seam allowance. Add the top and bottom border pieces in the same way, and mitre the corners (see Finishing Corners, page 9). Appliqué the balloons and kite into place.

4 Press the completed quilt top and the backing fabric. Lay the backing right side down, add the wadding (batting) and the pieced top to make a quilt sandwich. Use safety pins or tacking (basting) to hold the three layers together.

5 Cut a template for the quilting pattern marked on Template 3 using template plastic and carefully cutting round the curved lines. Transfer this pattern to all the blue squares, alternately reversing it to create a wavy pattern. Quilt the marked lines and around each doll. Quilt the hearts marked on Ruby and Laura's dresses.

6 Bind the quilt around all four sides and hem stitch in place on the wrong side. Add a label saying when and for whom the quilt was made.

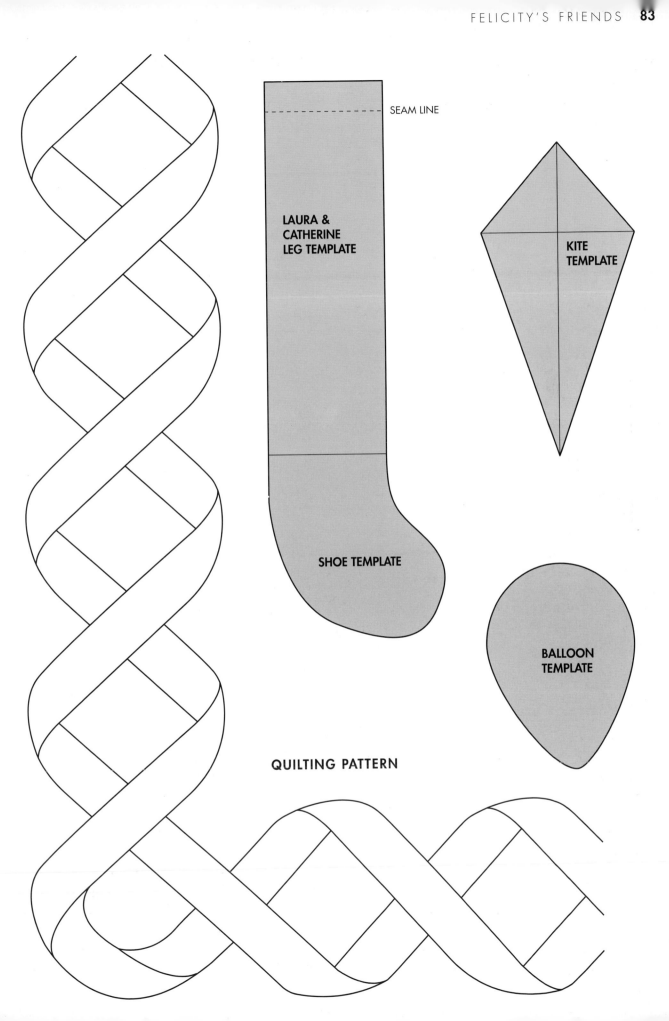

SEAM LINE

LAURA & CATHERINE LEG TEMPLATE

KITE TEMPLATE

SHOE TEMPLATE

BALLOON TEMPLATE

QUILTING PATTERN

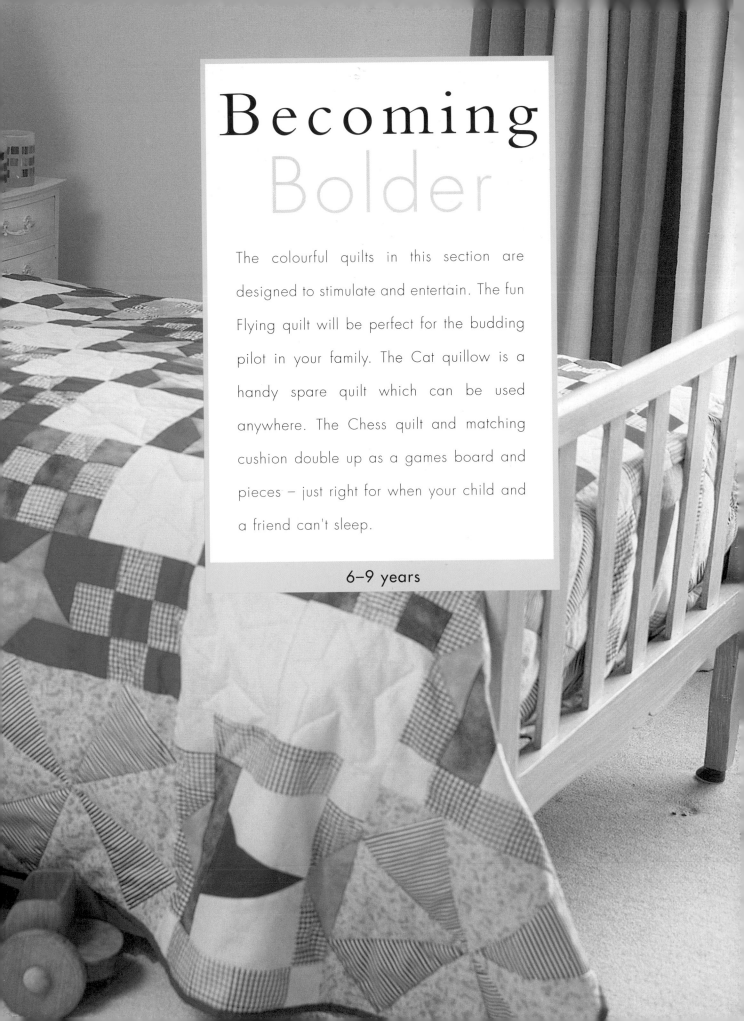

Becoming
Bolder

The colourful quilts in this section are designed to stimulate and entertain. The fun Flying quilt will be perfect for the budding pilot in your family. The Cat quillow is a handy spare quilt which can be used anywhere. The Chess quilt and matching cushion double up as a games board and pieces – just right for when your child and a friend can't sleep.

6–9 years

FLYING QUILT

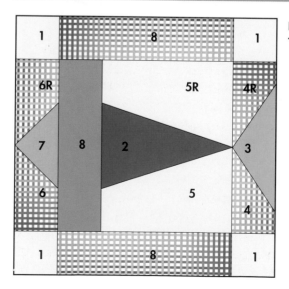

Here's the ideal quilt to make for a budding aviator. It is pieced from four different blocks, three of which have a flying theme. There are Propellers for movement, Friendship Stars to represent the sky, and my own special aeroplane block, Lane's Plane, that I based on an old bi-plane. This cheerful quilt will brighten up every room, and will still be popular when a young pilot takes his first flight.

1 Wash and press all the fabrics.

2 Trace off and make Lane's Plane Templates 1–8 on pages 91, 92 and 93 (see Seam Allowance Rule, page 7). Cut out the following pieces (see Rotary Cutting, page 7, and Machine Piecing, page 8):

48 x Template 1 in pale blue
12 x Template 2 in red
12 x Template 3 in dark yellow
12 x Template 4 in checked fabric
12 x Template 4R in checked fabric
12 x Template 5 in pale blue
12 x template 5R in pale blue
12 x Template 6 in checked fabric
12 x Template 6R in checked fabric
12 x Template 7 in dark yellow
12 x template 8 in green
24 x Template 8 in checked fabric

3 Piece the first Lane's Plane block together following the numbered order on the exploded block piecing diagram on page 89 and using a 5mm (¼in) seam allowance throughout. Make 11 more Lane's Plane blocks in the same way and lay them all to one side.

4 Trace off and make the Propeller Templates 1–3 on pages 89 and 91. Cut out the following pieces:

48 x Template 1 in striped fabric
48 x Template 2 in mottled blue fabric
48 x Template 3 in mottled blue fabric

FINISHED SIZE 244 x 183cm (96 x72in)
BLOCK SIZE Lane's Plane and Propeller: 30.5cm (12in)
Ninepatch and Friendship: 15cm (6in)

YOU WILL NEED
♦ Dark blue fabric, 50cm (½yd) by 112cm (44in)
♦ Red fabric, 50cm (½yd) by 112cm (44in)
♦ Orange fabric, 50cm (½yd) by 112cm (44in)
♦ Green fabric, 50cm (½yd) by 112cm (44in)
♦ Multi-coloured checked fabric, 1m (1yd) by 112cm (44in)
♦ Pale blue fabric, 2m (2yds) by 112cm (44in)
♦ Mottled blue fabric, 50cm (½yd) by 112cm (44in)
♦ Blue striped fabric, 50cm (½yd) by 112cm (44in)
♦ Fabric for backing, 5.5m (5½yds) by 112cm (44in)
♦ 2oz wadding (batting), 247 x 186cm (97 x 73in)
♦ Blue bias binding, 9.5m (9½yds) by 2.5cm (1in)
♦ Quilting thread

Use a 5mm (¼in) seam allowance throughout

LANE'S PLANE TEMPLATE KEY

5 Piece the first Propeller block together following the numbered order on the exploded block piecing diagram on page 89 and using a 5mm (¼in) seam allowance throughout. Make 11 more Propeller blocks in the same way and lay them all to one side.

6 Trace off and make Templates 1 and 2 on page 91 for the Ninepatch and Friendship Star centre panel. Cut the following pieces:
   147 x Template 1 in dark blue
   63 x Template 1 in dark yellow
   116 x Template 1 in checked fabric
   40 x Template 1 in green
   35 x Template 1 in red
   112 x Template 2 in dark blue
   112 x Template 2 in dark yellow
You will also need to cut 39 pale blue squares using the Plain Template on page 90.

7 Piece the first Friendship Star block together in dark yellow and blue following the numbered order on the exploded block piecing diagram on page 89 and using a 5mm (¼in) seam allowance throughout. Make 27 more Friendship Star blocks in the same way and lay them all to one side.

QUILT PIECING DIAGRAM

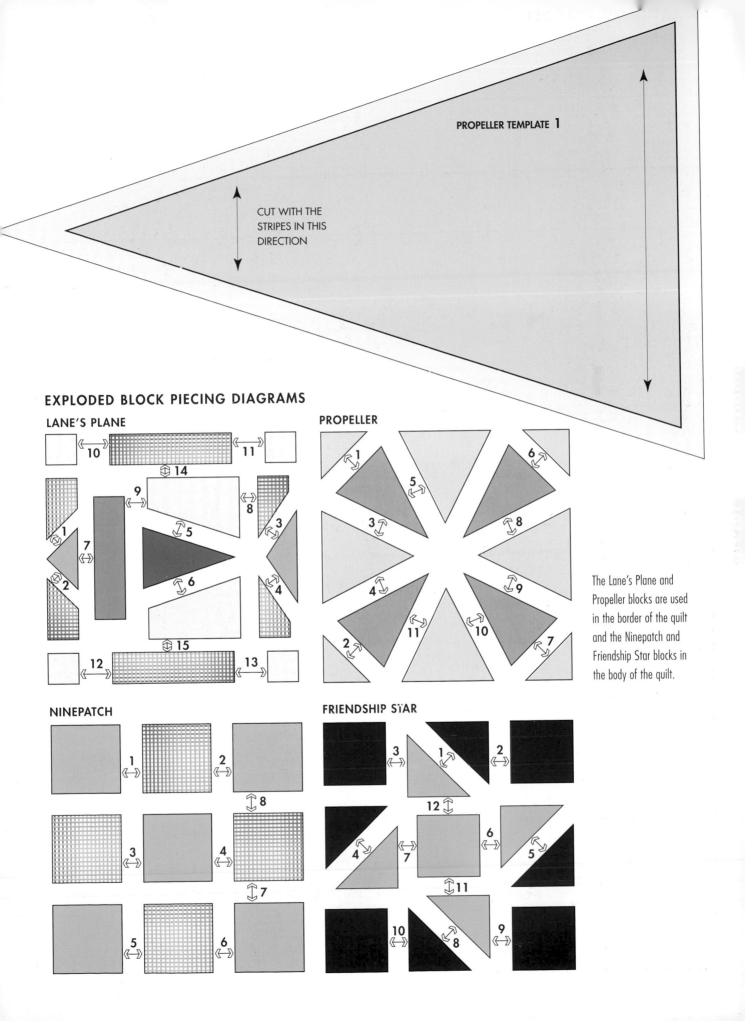

PROPELLER TEMPLATE 1

CUT WITH THE
STRIPES IN THIS
DIRECTION

EXPLODED BLOCK PIECING DIAGRAMS

LANE'S PLANE

PROPELLER

The Lane's Plane and
Propeller blocks are used
in the border of the quilt
and the Ninepatch and
Friendship Star blocks in
the body of the quilt.

NINEPATCH

FRIENDSHIP STAR

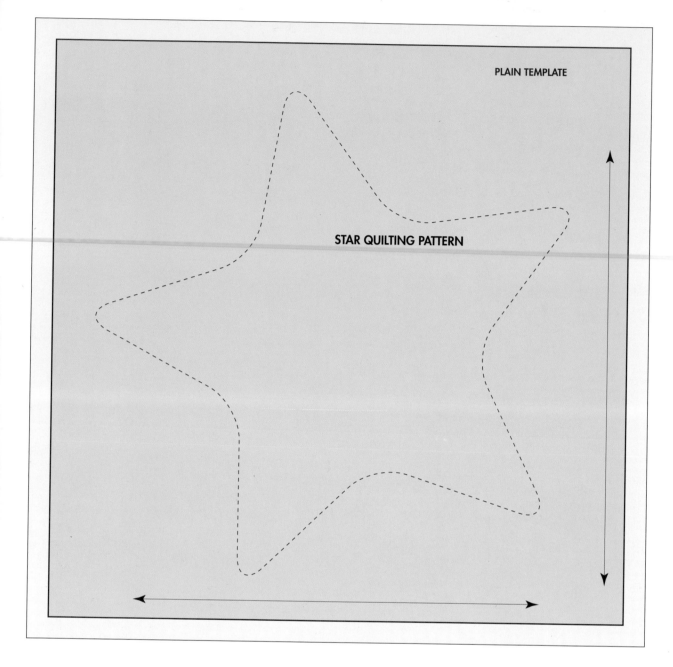

PLAIN TEMPLATE

STAR QUILTING PATTERN

8 Piece the Ninepatch blocks together following the numbered order of the exploded block piecing diagram on page 89 and using a 5mm (¼in) seam allowance throughout as follows:

7 in dark yellow and checked fabric
8 in green and checked fabric
7 in red and checked fabric
7 in dark blue and checked fabric

9 Using the quilt piecing diagram on page 88 as a guide, join the Ninepatch, Friendship Star and plain blue blocks into 12 strips of eight blocks. Join these strips together to form the centre panel of the quilt.

10 Join two Lane's Plane blocks to two Propeller blocks as shown in the quilt piecing diagram to make a strip of four and sew this with right sides together to the top of the centre panel. Make a second strip of four blocks and attach this to the bottom of the centre panel. Join the remaining Lane's Plane and Propeller blocks into strips of eight and stitch one to each side of the centre panel.

11 Press the completed quilt top. Cut your backing fabric in half across the width. Join the two strips along the selvedge edge to make the backing piece.

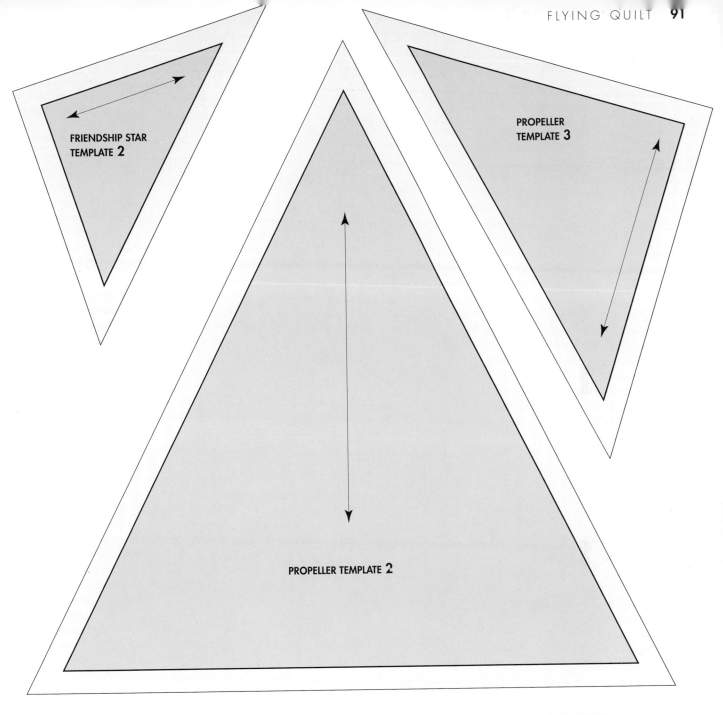

FRIENDSHIP STAR
TEMPLATE **2**

PROPELLER
TEMPLATE **3**

PROPELLER TEMPLATE **2**

12 Mark a star in each of the plain blue squares using the star quilting pattern opposite.

13 Lay the backing face down with the wadding (batting) and pieced quilt on top to form a quilt sandwich. Use safety pins or tacking (basting) to hold the three layers together.

14 Outline quilt all the patchwork blocks and quilt the stars.

15 Bind with the bias binding (see Binding, page 9).

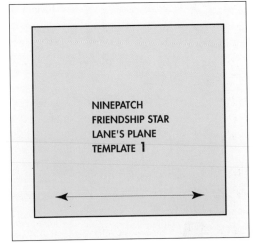

NINEPATCH
FRIENDSHIP STAR
LANE'S PLANE
TEMPLATE **1**

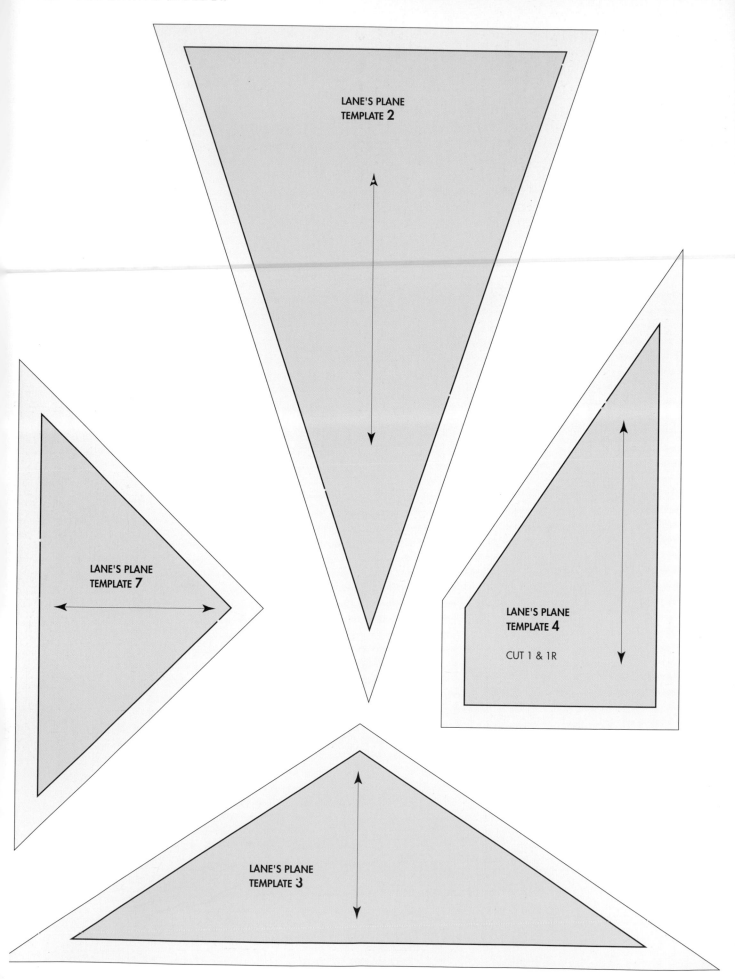

LANE'S PLANE
TEMPLATE 2

LANE'S PLANE
TEMPLATE 7

LANE'S PLANE
TEMPLATE 4

CUT 1 & 1R

LANE'S PLANE
TEMPLATE 3

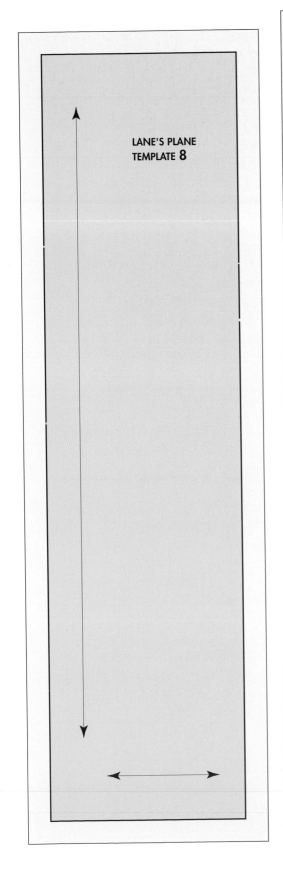

LANE'S PLANE
TEMPLATE 8

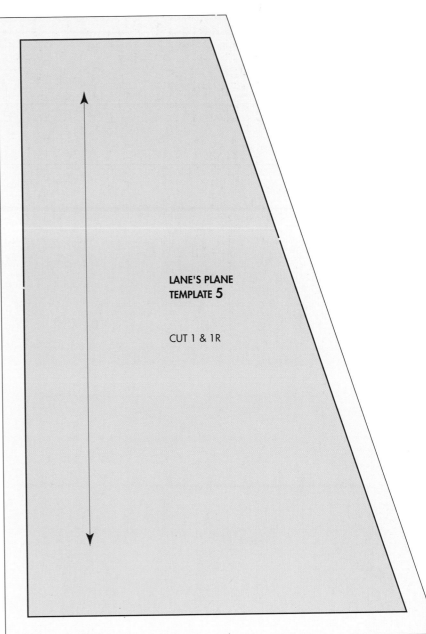

LANE'S PLANE
TEMPLATE 5

CUT 1 & 1R

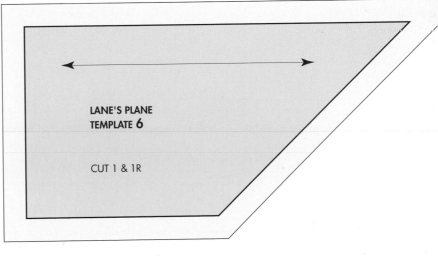

LANE'S PLANE
TEMPLATE 6

CUT 1 & 1R

THE CHESS QUILT

This striking chequerboard quilt decorated with stencilled chess pieces is both attractive and practical because you can actually use the squares to play chess or draughts across its top. The chess pieces are made from matching fabric and stored in a cushion, making this an ideal quilt to take on a family holiday.

TO MAKE THE QUILT

1 Wash and press all the fabrics.

2 From the plain red fabric, cut two 254 x 6.35cm (100 x 2½in) strips and two 40 x 165cm (15½ x 65in) strips. Lay to one side.

3 From each fabric cut 32 x 21.6cm (8½in) squares. This can be done using a rotary cutter and ruler (see Rotary Cutting, page 7), or a template made from card or plastic.

4 Following the piecing diagram on page 96, join the red and checked squares in strips of eight, then join the eight resulting strips as shown.

5 Join the wider strips of red fabric to opposite edges of the square with right sides together and press. Join a long red strip to each long edge of the quilt and press.

6 Enlarge the chess piece stencils on page 97 by 100% on a photocopier. Either trace each design on to template plastic or glue the photocopy to cardboard. Cut these out for the stencils leaving at least 8cm (3in) around the outlines. Carefully cut round the drawn lines using a craft knife.

7 Using the piecing diagram as a guide, and following the instructions for your fabric paint, stencil the pieces at each end of the quilt. I inverted half of the designs so that whichever end you are playing from you can see the pieces the right way up.

8 Leave plenty of time for the paint to dry before ironing the whole quilt from the wrong side.

9 Cut the backing fabric in half, and join two selvage edges to create a large piece. Press.

10 Mark the quilting pattern on page 98 in each of the red squares and two diagonal lines in each of the checked squares.

11 Lay the backing face down and put the wadding (batting) and pieced quilt on top to form a quilt sandwich. Use safety pins or tacking (basting) to hold the three layers together. Quilt around the marked lines and the chess pieces.

12 Bind the quilt using the bias binding (see Binding, page 9).

FINISHED SIZE
254 x 178cm (100 x 70in)

YOU WILL NEED
- Red checked fabric, 3m (3yds) by 112cm (44in) wide fabric
- Blue checked fabric, 1m (1yd) by 112cm (44in) wide fabric
- Plain red fabric, 3.5m (3½yds) by 112cm (44in) wide fabric
- Backing fabric, 5.5m (5½yds) by 112cm (44in) wide fabric
- 2oz wadding (batting), 260 x 183cm (102 x 72in)
- Blue bias binding, 8m (8yds) by 2.5cm (1in) wide
- Fabric paint and stencil brush (see Suppliers, page 127)
- Template plastic
- Polystyrene beads – available from pet shops
- One 18cm (7in) zip to match the board background fabric
- Matching sewing cotton
- White quilting thread

A 5mm (¼in) seam allowance is used throughout

QUILT PIECING DIAGRAM

CHESS PIECE STENCILS

QUILTING PATTERN

TO MAKE THE CHESS PIECES

1 Cut 32 x 11.5cm (4½in) squares from the red checked fabric and 32 x 11.5cm (4½in) squares from the blue checked fabric.

2 Cut six 10cm (4in) squares in template plastic. Using a fine black permanent marker, trace the chess pieces on page 97 on to template plastic. Carefully cut out around the marked chess pieces using a craft knife.

3 Stencil the following on to both the red and blue fabrics: eight pawns, two castles, two knights, two bishops, one king and one queen. Allow the paint to dry and press.

4 Place a stencilled square right sides together with an unstencilled square of the same colour. Sew around the edges using a 5mm (¼in) seam allowance and leaving a 5cm (2in) opening in the fourth side.

5 Turn each bag to the right side smoothing the corners and the seams with a knitting needle.

6 Stuff each bag with polystyrene beads. Pin the opening of each bag shut and oversew this when all the bags have been filled.

TO MAKE A CUSHION

1 To make a cushion in which to store the chess pieces, cut two 35cm (13½in) squares from the leftover plain red fabric.

2 Place the two pieces right sides together and sew along one edge, using a long machine stitch and a 5mm (¼in) seam allowance.

3 Press the seam open and pin the zip about half way along the seam. Using the zipper foot, sew the zip in place with two or three bars at each end. Using a seam ripper cut the stitches the length of the zip. Open the zip an inch or two.

4 Put the two pieces right sides together again and sew around the remaining three sides.

5 Open the zip fully and turn the cushion to the right side. Press.

CAT QUILLOW

This clever quilt design can be folded away into a stylish cushion when it is not needed, making it ideal for stowing in the back of the car or caravan or on a spare bed. I came across many cat fabrics while I was looking for fabrics for the Storytime quilt and I couldn't resist buying some. The quilt is made from squares of these fabrics and the cushion is decorated with a watchful appliquéd cat.

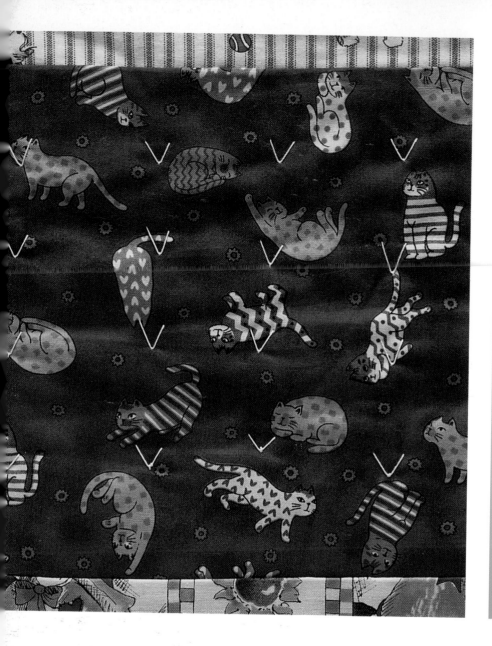

FINISHED SIZE

Quilt: 163 x 142cm (64 x 56in)
Cushion: 51 x 46cm (20 x 18in)

YOU WILL NEED

FOR THE QUILT:

◆ 56 x 21.6cm (8½in) squares of fabric
◆ Fabric for backing, 3m (3yds) by 112cm (44in) wide
◆ 2oz wadding (batting), 165 x 145cm (65 x 57in)
◆ White quilting thread
◆ Bias binding, 7m (7yds) by 2.5cm (1in) wide

A 5mm (¼in) seam allowance is used throughout

FOR THE CUSHION:

◆ Fabric for the cat, 25cm (¼yd) by 112cm (44in) wide
◆ Fabric for the background, 25cm (¼yd) by 112cm (44in) wide
◆ Backing fabric, 25cm (¼yd) by 112cm (44in) wide
◆ 2oz wadding (batting), 54 x 49cm (21 x 19in)
◆ Scraps of fabric for bib and ears
◆ Black and brown stranded cotton (floss)
◆ Two buttons for eyes

TO MAKE THE QUILT

1 Join seven of the squares to make a strip using a 5mm (¼in) seam allowance and pressing the seams to one side.

2 Make seven further strips, pressing the seams in the opposite direction each time. This will make it easier to sew the strips together.

3 Join the first two strips with right sides together and nestling the seams together. Push a pin long-ways into each seam junction and sew the strips together using a 5mm (¼in) seam allowance.

4 Join the rest of the strips in the same way and press the completed quilt top.

5 Cut one metre (one yard) from the three-metre (three-yard) length of backing fabric. Cut this in half lengthways and join the short ends. Sew this strip, right sides together, to the selvage edge of the two-metre (two-yard) length. Press.

6 Place the backing piece right side down and put the wadding (batting) and pieced quilt right side up on top. Pin with safety pins or tack (baste) the three layers together to make a quilt sandwich.

7 Quilt using chicken scratch quilting (see page 10).

8 Bind the quilt using the bias binding (see Binding, page 9).

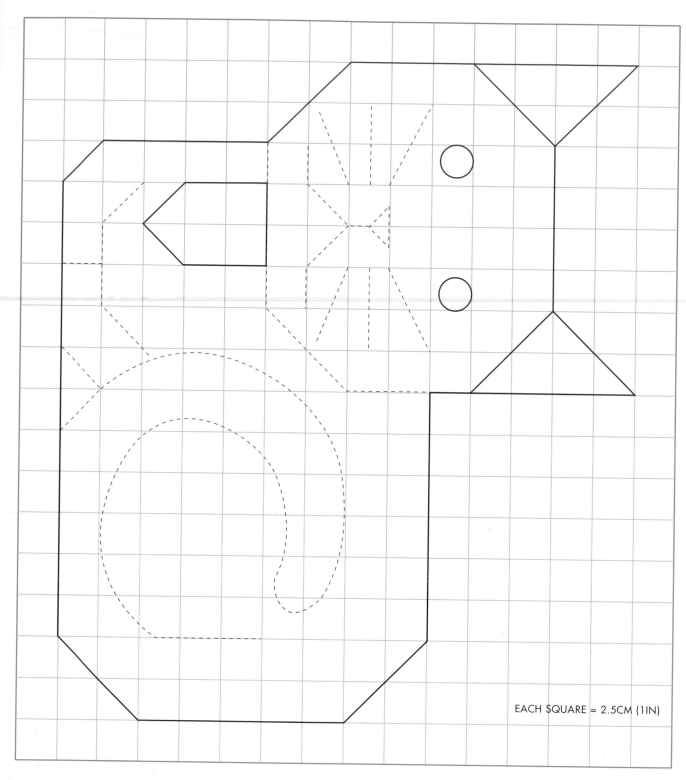

EACH SQUARE = 2.5CM (1IN)

**APPLIQUÉ TEMPLATE
AND QUILTING PATTERN**

TO MAKE THE CUSHION

1 Copy the cat appliqué pattern opposite onto 2.5cm (1in) squared paper and use it to make templates for the cat's body, ears, bib and face.

2 Cut out the cat's body and the bib leaving a 5mm (¼in) seam allowance. Turn under a 5mm (¼in) hem on all the edges of the bib except for the top. Hem stitch the bib in place on the cat's body. Using a light surface such as a window, mark the tail and face quilting designs: white pencil may show up best.

3 Cut out the cat's ears and face, leaving a 5mm (¼in) seam allowance. Stitch the ears to the face, and then the face to the body. Mark the quilting pattern onto the finished appliqué with white pencil.

4 Turn under a 5mm (¼in) seam around the whole piece, and tack (baste) down.

5 Press the background fabric, and centre the cat on it. Pin and hem stitch in place.

6 Lay the scrap fabric, wadding (batting) and cat together and pin or tack (baste) to form a quilt sandwich.

7 Quilt the outline of the tail and paws using stem stitch. Quilt around the bib and the entire cat outline.

8 Sew the nose in satin stitch, and the whiskers in stem stitch. Add the button eyes.

9 Place the backing fabric right sides together with the completed cat. Pin.

10 Stitch around four sides, using a 5mm (¼in) seam allowance and leaving a 15cm (6in) opening for turning on one side.

11 Turn to the right side using a knitting needle to push the corners out straight. Hem stitch the opening together.

12 Quilt a line 5mm (¼in) from the edge all around the sewn pieces.

TO COMPLETE THE QUILLOW

1 Fold the quilt into three, with the back facing you.

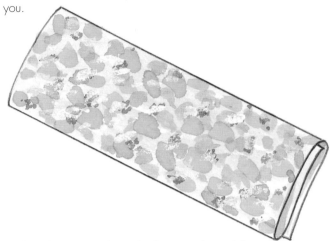

2 Place the cat panel upside down on the middle third and pin in place.

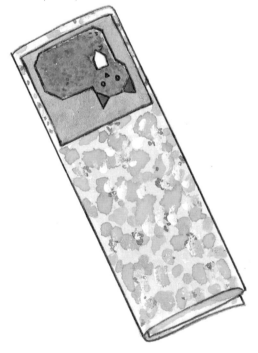

3 Hem stitch around the two sides and the top of the cat panel.

4 Fold the cat down so that it is now the right way up.

5 Fold the rest of the quilt over itself, then tuck it into the cat as shown right.

Into the
Future

Each of the quilts in this chapter is designed to be used at any stage of life. The Starcross quilt and Tam's Patch have a rugged appearance, whilst the Ribbon Star quilt's jewel-like colours will cheer any room. The Christmas Log Cabin quilt evokes the warmth and cosiness of Christmas, and everybody needs a Christmas stocking, don't they?

10–13 years

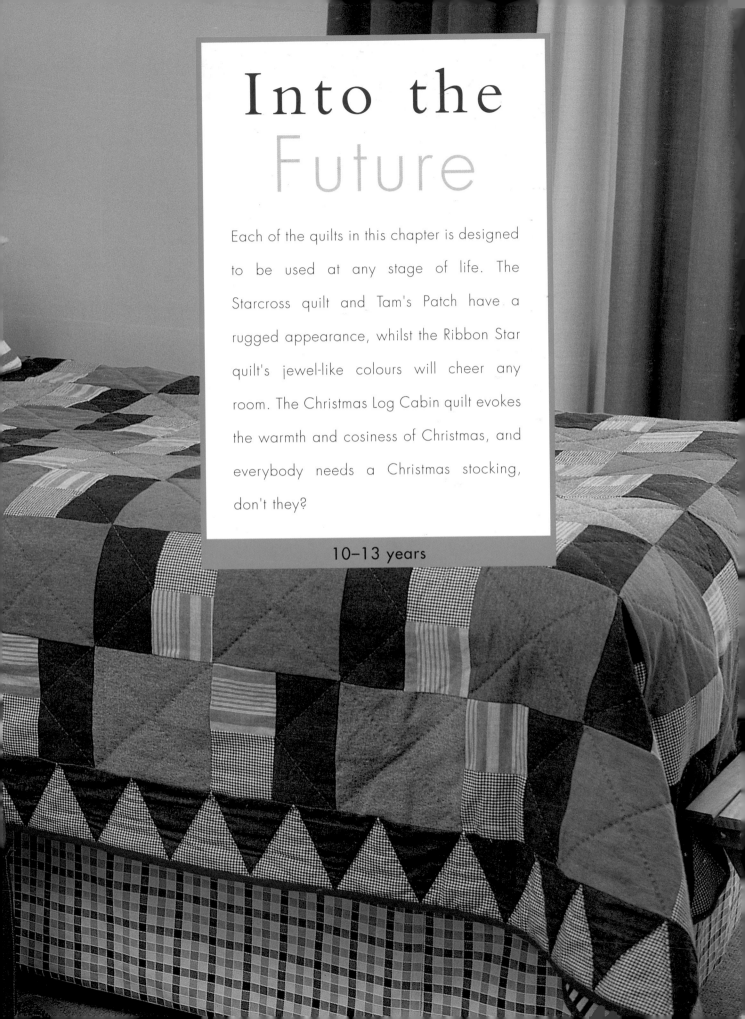

TAM'S PATCH QUILT

This quilt shows just how resourceful we quilters can be – it's made from pairs of old jeans and an old chambray shirt. This fabric makes the quilt both warm and durable, and likely to appeal to a teenager. The design is straightforward to piece and uses patterned fabrics to contrast with the denim. A matching cushion will add a stylish finishing touch to your teenager's bedroom.

As denim is such a thick fabric, you will find it much easier to cut out the pieces for this quilt using a rotary cutter (see Rotary Cutting, page 7) and to sew them on a sewing machine (see Machine Piecing, page 8).

TO MAKE THE QUILT

1 Wash, iron and dismantle each pair of jeans and lay them to one side.

2 Trace off and make Templates A–F on pages 108–109 (see Seam Allowance Rule, page 7). To make both the quilt and the cushion, cut the following pieces:

- 72 x Template A in darker denim
- 72 x Template B in red stripes
- 72 x Template B in blue checks
- 72 x Template C in lighter denim
- 8 x Template D in red stripes (4 for the quilt and 4 for the cushion)
- 76 x Template E in darker denim
- 96 x Template E in blue checks
- 8 x Template F in darker denim
- 8 x Template FR in darker denim

3 Stitch a small red striped square to a blue checked square, then add a denim square one end and a denim rectangle at the other end as shown on the left. Make 69 further blocks in this way.

4 Join the blocks into seven strips of ten, arranging them as shown in the quilting and piecing diagram opposite. Press the seams on half of the strips to one side, and on the other half to the other side.

5 Join the strips together, pinning the seam junctions together as shown in the diagram on page 40 to prevent the seams from slipping and distorting the patchwork.

6 Join the denim and blue checked triangles (E). Make two strips 41 triangles long and two strips 29 triangles long in this way for the quilt border. Add an F and an F(R) denim triangle at either end of each strip to straighten the edge. Add a large red striped square to each end of the longer strip. Sew the two shorter strips to the top and bottom of the quilt, then add the longer strips to both sides of the quilt. Press the completed quilt top.

7 Piece the backing fabric together and press the seams.

8 Lay the backing face down and put the wadding (batting) and pieced quilt on top to form a quilt sandwich. Use safety pins or tacking (basting) to hold the three layers together.

9 Quilt following the design shown in the quilting and piecing diagram opposite.

10 Bind the quilt using the red bias binding (see Binding, page 9).

TO MAKE THE CUSHION

1 Make and join two blocks as described in step 3 opposite. For the borders, make four strips 5 triangles long as described in step 6 opposite. Finish each strip by stitching an F and an F(R) denim triangle to either end. Add a red square to each end of two of the strips. Stitch the shorter strips to two edges of the cushion, then the longer strips to the other two sides. Press the completed top.

2 Cut off the sleeves and the back from the chambray shirt. Place the cushion top right sides together with the front of the shirt. Cut a square from the shirt. If the front is not big enough, add extra fabric all round from the sleeves.

3 Pin and sew the shirt front to the cushion top, sewing the seams twice for extra strength. Undo the buttons and turn the cushion through to the right side, pushing out the four corners. Insert the cushion pad and do up the buttons.

QUILTING AND PIECING DIAGRAM

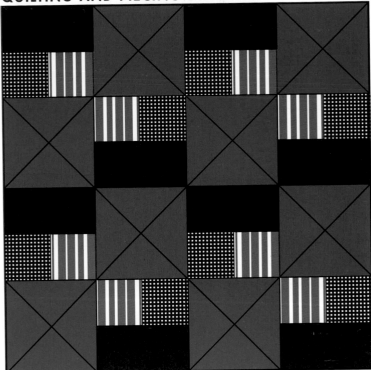

FINISHED SIZE
213 x 152cm (92 x 68in)

YOU WILL NEED
- At least 10 pairs of old denim jeans
- Blue checked fabric, 1m (1yd) by 112cm (44in) wide
- Red striped fabric, 1m (1yd) by 112cm (44in) wide or an old shirt
- Fabric for backing, 1.25m (1¼yds) by 112cm (44in) wide
- 2oz wadding (batting), 216 x155cm (85 x 61in)
- Red bias binding, 8m (8yds) by 2.5cm (1in) wide
- An old chambray shirt to finish the cushion
- 46cm (18in) cushion pad

Use a 5mm (¼in) seam allowance throughout

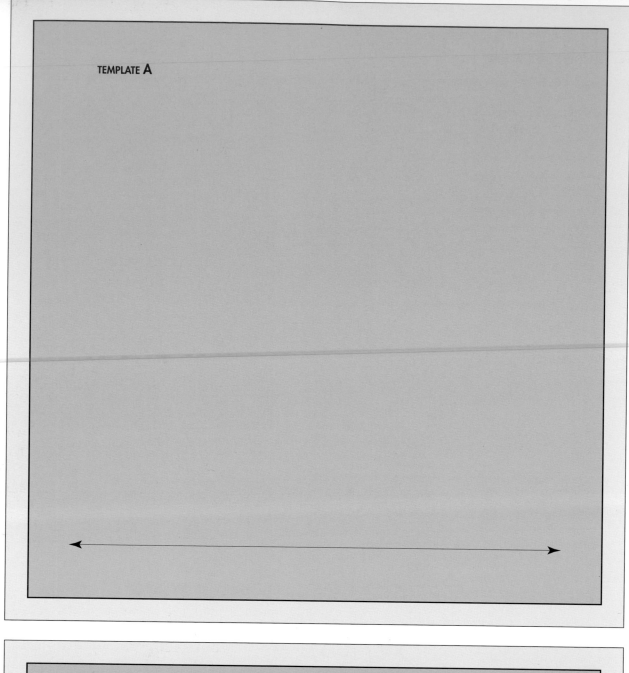

TEMPLATE A

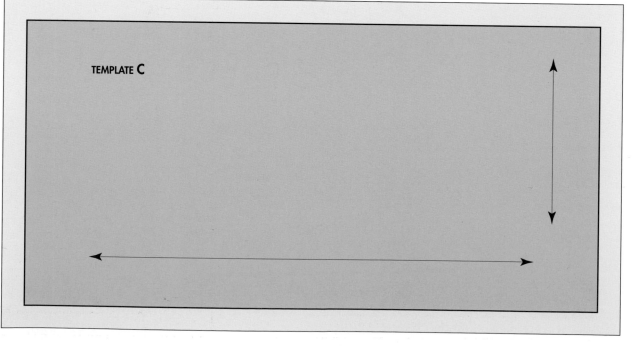

TEMPLATE C

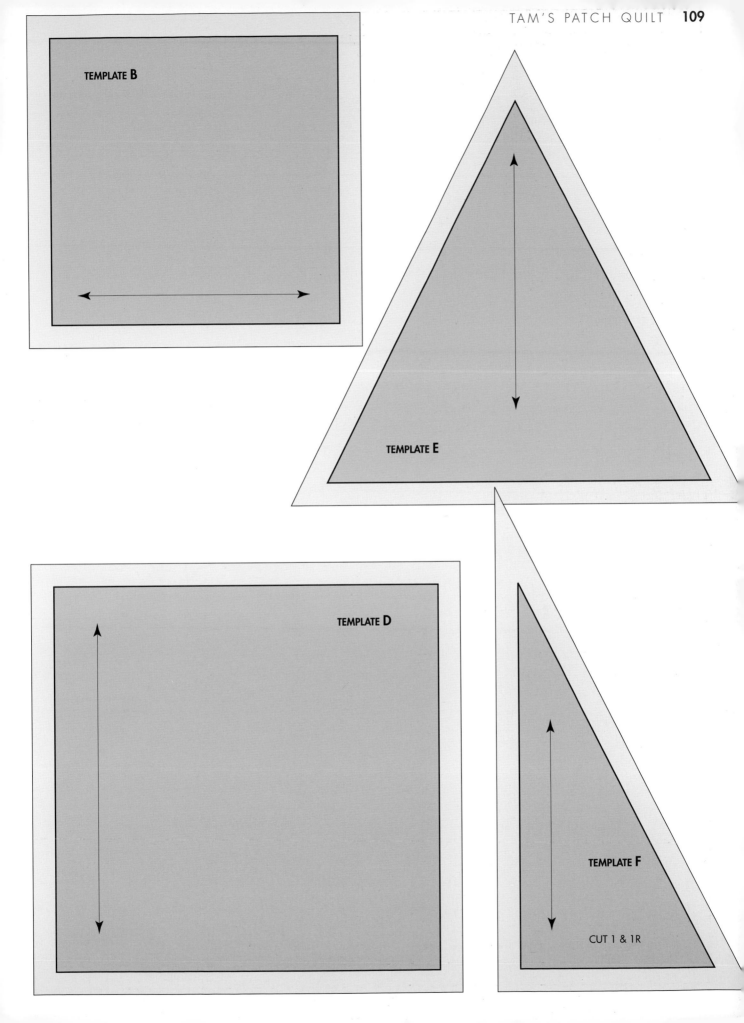

TEMPLATE B

TEMPLATE E

TEMPLATE D

TEMPLATE F

CUT 1 & 1R

STARCROSS QUILT

When you receive a request for a quilt from a special godson, you must listen carefully to what he wants, then do your best to make a quilt that will accompany him through life. This Starcross quilt is the result. The muted red and blue checked fabric lends itself well to this pleasing quilt design.

FINISHED SIZE
185cm x 231cm (73in x 91in)

YOU WILL NEED
- Denim fabric (fabric 1), 2m (2yds) by 112cm (44in) wide
- Red fabric (fabric 2), 1.5m (1½yds) by 112cm (44in) wide
- Beige fabric (fabric 3), 1.5m (1½yds) by 112cm (44in) wide
- Checked fabric (fabric 4), 5m (5yds) by 112cm (44in) wide
- 2oz wadding (batting), 188 x 233cm (74 x 92in)
- Dark red quilting thread

A 5mm (¼in) seam allowance is used throughout

1 Wash and press all the fabrics.

2 Trace off and make Templates A–D on pages 114–115 (see Seam Allowance Rule, page 7). Cut out the following pieces (see Rotary Cutting, page 7, and Machine Piecing, page 8):
- 160 x Template A in fabric 1
- 160 x Template A in fabric 2
- 76 x Template A in fabric 3
- 43 x Template B in fabric 4
- 4 x Template D in fabric 4
- 32 x Template C in fabric 4
Take care to follow the grain line.

3 Using the quilt piecing diagram opposite as a guide, make the strips as follows:

ROW ONE: Sew two A pieces to each C piece. Join these blocks into a strip with a D piece at each end.

ROW TWO: Make four pinwheel blocks using the A pieces, and three 'square within a square' blocks using the A and B pieces. Join these together in a strip and add an extra C and 2 A pieces at each end.

ROW THREE: Make seven 'square within a square' blocks. Add an extra C and 2 A pieces at each end.

EXPLODED BLOCK PIECING DIAGRAMS

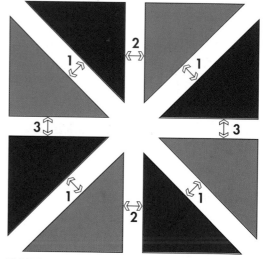

PINWHEEL

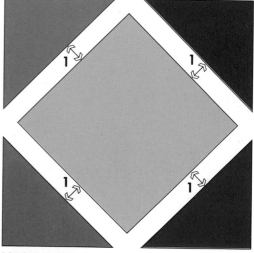

SQUARE WITHIN A SQUARE

QUILT PIECING DIAGRAM

ROW 1

ROW 2

ROW 3

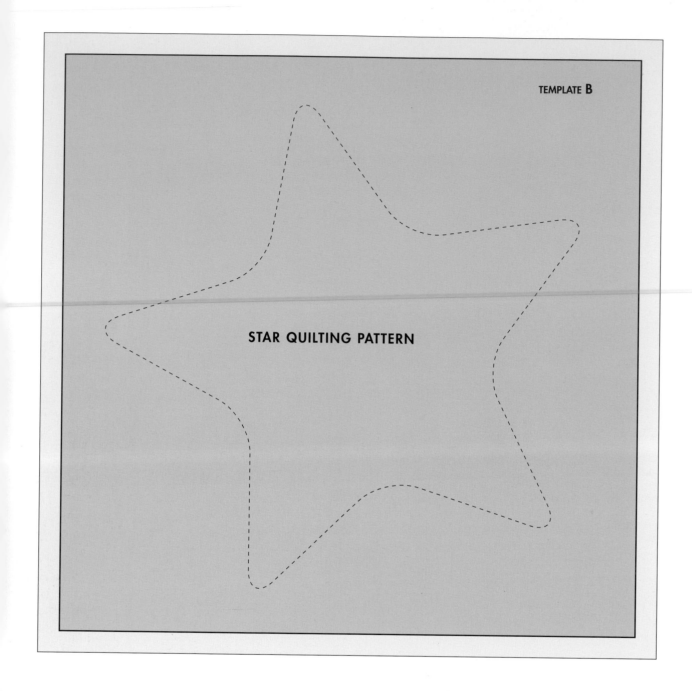

TEMPLATE **B**

STAR QUILTING PATTERN

Make 2 x Row One, 5 x Row Two and 4 x Row Three. Join them together in the order shown on the quilt piecing diagram (see page 40 for pressing and pinning the seams together). Press the completed quilt top.

4 Cut two pieces of checked fabric two metres (two yards) long. Join them selvage to selvage to make the quilt backing and press the seam open.

5 Lay the backing right side down, put the wadding (batting) and the pieced quilt on top to make a quilt sandwich. Use safety pins or tacking (basting) to hold the three layers together.

6 Outline quilt all the seams approx. 5mm (¼in) away from the sewn line.

7 Transfer the star quilting pattern above on to the centre of all the squares. Quilt all around the marked star shape.

8 Bind the quilt (see Binding, page 9) with straight strips cut from the denim fabric.

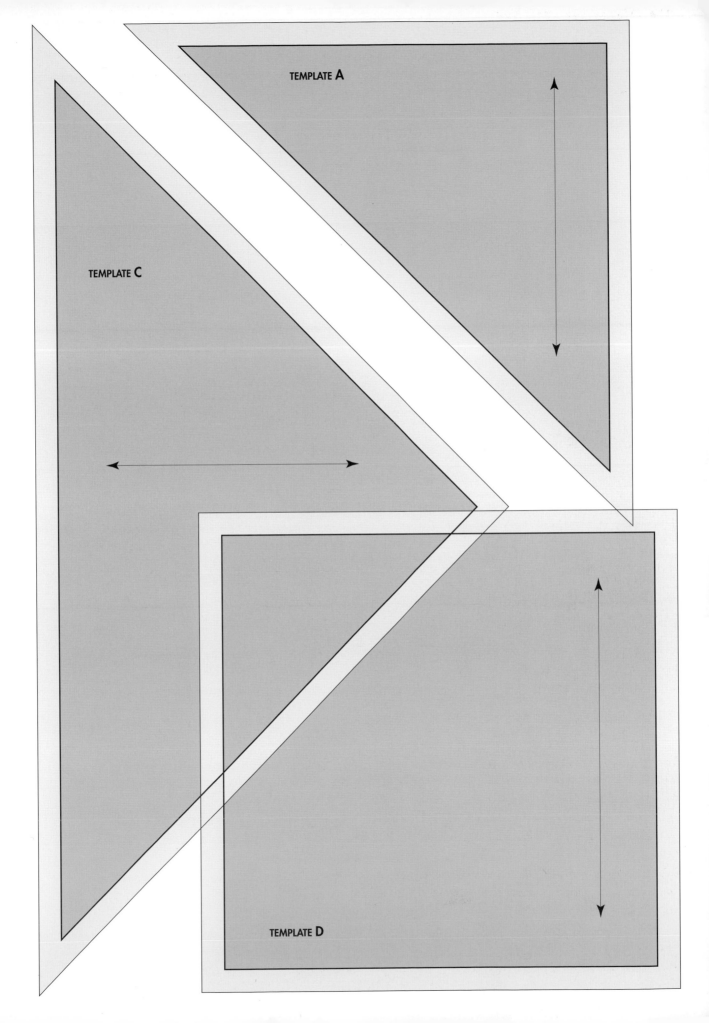

TEMPLATE **A**

TEMPLATE **C**

TEMPLATE **D**

RIBBON STAR QUILT

This gorgeous quilt is made from a very simple block that requires only two templates. The design is brought to life by the rich fabrics it is made from. These are in seven colours of the rainbow and are used here to form a stunning ribbon and star design.

FINISHED SIZE 234cm x 173cm (92 x 68in)
BLOCK SIZE 30.5cm (12in)

YOU WILL NEED
- Five different rainbow fabrics, 50cm (½yd) of each by 112cm (44in) wide
- Blue fabric, 5.5m (5½ yds) by 112cm (44in) wide
- Dark blue fabric, 1.5m (1½yds) by 112cm (44in) wide for binding
- Purple fabric, 2m (2yds) by 112cm (44in) wide
- 2oz wadding (batting), 236 x 178cm (93 x 70in)
- Matching quilting thread

A 5mm (¼in) seam allowance is used throughout

EXPLODED BLOCK PIECING DIAGRAM

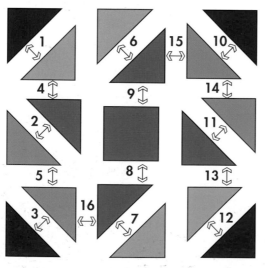

1 Wash and press all the fabrics. From the blue fabric, cut two 234 x 11.5cm (92 x 4½in) pieces, and two 193 x 11.5cm (76 x 4½in) pieces for the wider, outer border. From the dark blue fabric cut two 150cm (60in) x 7.5cm (1½in) pieces, and two 210cm (84in) x 7.5cm (1½in) pieces for the border. Trace off and make Templates A and B on page 120 (see Seam Allowance Rule, page 7). Cut out the following pieces (see Rotary Cutting, page 7, and Machine Piecing, page 8):

  9 x Template A and 24 x Template B pieces in each of the rainbow colours
  148 x Template B in dark blue
  68 x Template B in blue
  168 x Template B in purple

2 Piece the first block together following the numbered order on the exploded block piecing diagram below left and using a 5mm (¼in) seam allowance throughout. Make 34 more blocks in the same way.

3 To make the inner border, join the shorter border strips to the top and bottom of the pieced quilt and the longer ones to each side. Mitre the corners (see Finishing Corners, page 9). Make the inner border in the same way. Press the completed quilt top.

4 Lay the backing face down with the wadding (batting) and pieced quilt on top to form a quilt sandwich ready for quilting.

QUILT PIECING DIAGRAM

5 Bind the quilt using 2.5cm (1in) strips cut from the dark blue fabric.

QUILTING NOTE

I sent this quilt away to be professionally quilted on a Gammill Classic long arm quilting machine. The quilter chose motifs which perfectly complement the quilt some of which could be adapted for quilting on domestic machines. Practise on spare wadded fabric before starting to quilt the main piece. The designs were as follows.

LOOPIES This is a combination of o's and e's joined together which can be enlarged or reduced to fit any narrow borders.

LOOPY STARS Freehand five pointed stars joined with loops and ribbons, can be adjusted to fit borders or blocks.

CURLY FLOWER On a domestic machine it would be easier to complete one quarter of the design before rotating the quilt to complete the next segment.

LOOPY STARS

NOTE
The arrows show the direction of sewing

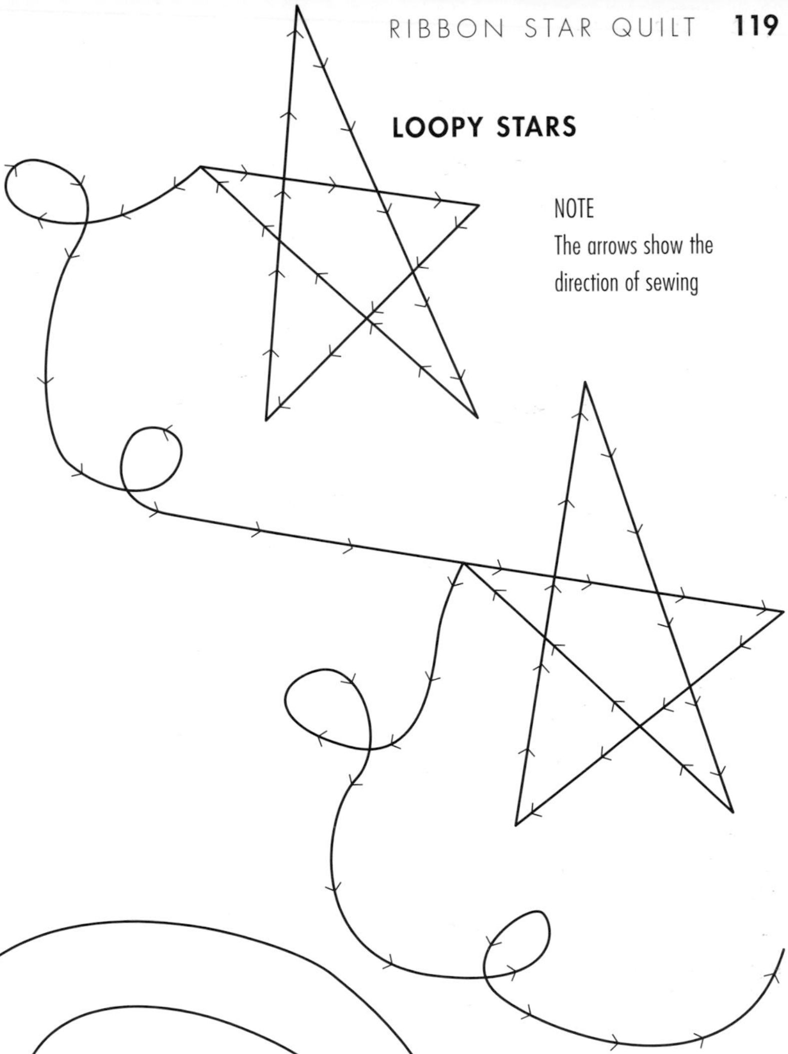

CURLY FLOWER

LOOPIES

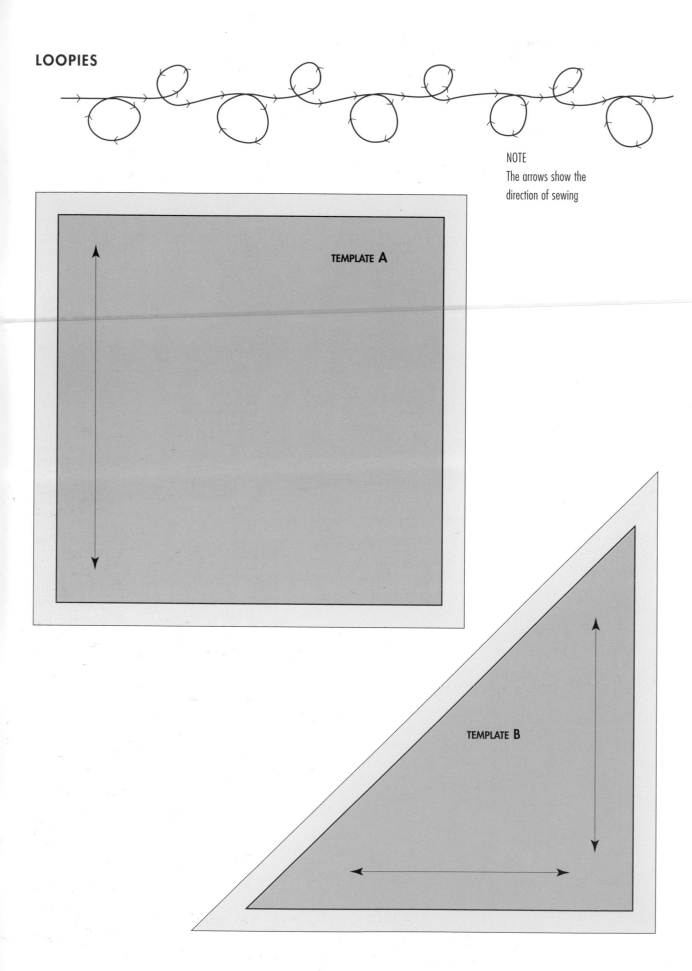

NOTE
The arrows show the
direction of sewing

TEMPLATE A

TEMPLATE B

CHRISTMAS LOG CABIN QUILT AND STOCKING

Quilts and Christmas seem to belong together. This log cabin quilt made from festive red and green fabrics would look lovely draped on a sofa or hung on a wall in a festively-decorated room. But it would look best of all spread out on a child's bed with the crazy patchwork Christmas stocking hanging at one end.

FINISHED SIZE 203 x 152cm (80 x 60in)

YOU WILL NEED

◆ Yellow fabric, 50cm (½yd) by 112cm (44in) wide
◆ Three red fabrics, 1m (1yd) of each by 112cm (44in) wide
◆ Three green fabrics, 1m (1yd) of each by 112cm (44in) wide
◆ Red patterned fabric, 5m (5yds) by 112cm (44in) wide for borders and backing
◆ Green patterned fabric, 5m (5yds) by 112cm (44in) wide for borders and backing
◆ 2oz wadding (batting), 158 x 208cm (62 x 82in)
◆ Red or green quilting thread

A 5mm (¼in) seam allowance is used throughout

TO MAKE THE QUILT

1 Wash and press all the fabrics. Mark out a square 76 x 76mm (3 x 3in) on to thick card and use as a template to cut out 48 centre squares in yellow.

2 Cut the other fabrics into 3.2cm (1¼in) strips across the width of the fabric (see Rotary Cutting, page 7). Lay them to one side.

3 Begin to piece a block. Take a yellow square and place the square right sides together with a red strip (strip1) and stitch. Trim the red strip level with the centre square, and press the seam away from the centre (see Fig1).

4 Take another red strip (strip 2) and join it to these pieces. Trim the strip so that it is level with the other fabrics and press as before (see Fig 2).

5 Stitch a green strip opposite the first red strip, trim and press. Add a second green strip to the fourth side of the yellow square (see Figs 3 and 4).

6 Add two more rounds of red and green strips to complete the block as shown, trimming the fabric and pressing the seams away from the centre as before.

7 Make another 47 blocks in this way. Join them together as shown in the quilt piecing diagram on page 124. Press the completed quilt top.

8 From the border fabric, cut two 216 x 14cm (85 x 5½in) strips and two 165 x 14cm (65 x 5½in) strips. Stitch the two longer strips to the sides of the quilt top, and the other two strips to the top and bottom edges.

9 Mark the quilting design on page 42 on the border.

10 Join the backing fabric together to make one piece and press. Lay it face down and put the wadding (batting) and then the pieced quilt on top to make a quilt sandwich. Use safety pins or tacking (batting) to hold the three layers together.

11 Quilt just inside the sewn line of each square of the block. Quilt the border design.

12 Neaten the edges of the quilt by turning under 5mm (¼in) all round on both the backing and the pieced quilt top. Quilt all round the edges, approx. 32mm (⅛in) in from the edge.

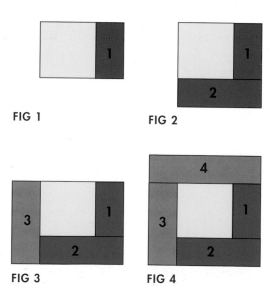

FIG 1

FIG 2

FIG 3

FIG 4

QUILT PIECING DIAGRAM

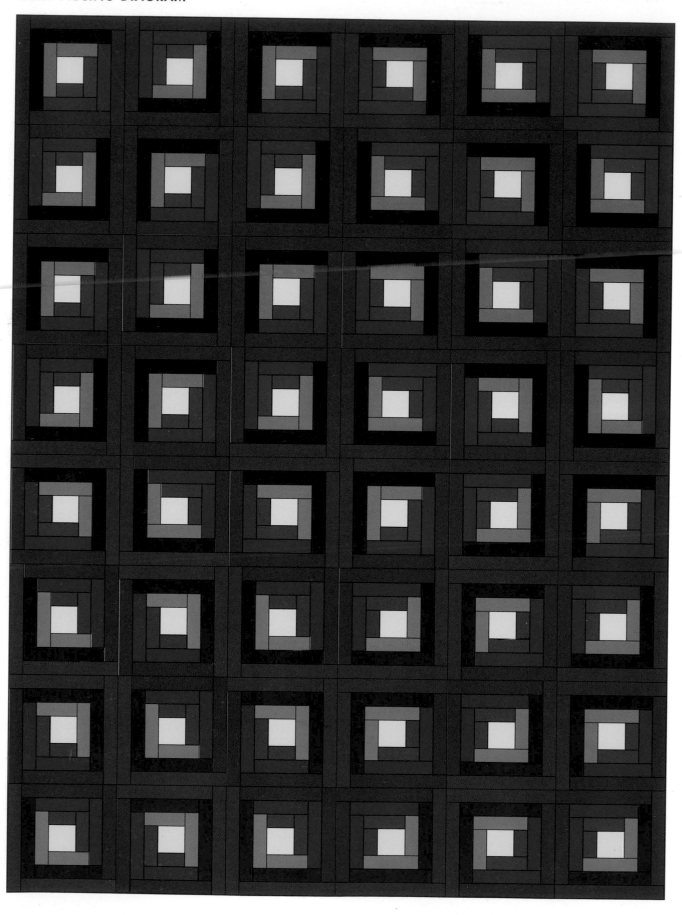

Personalise your stocking by adding a name if you wish. Cut the letters from fabric and attach to the stocking top with fusible bonding web

TO MAKE THE STOCKING

This crazy patchwork stocking is easy to make and, at 61cm (24in) long, will hold plenty of presents.

1 Decide which way you want the toe of your stocking to point. Then using the stocking pattern, Template A on page 126, cut the following pieces:

2 x lining fabric
1 x waste fabric
1 x backing fabric
2 x wadding (batting)

2 Lay the waste fabric flat on a table, and place one of the wadding (batting) pieces on top. Pin together all round the edge with safety pins.

3 With a ruler and a dark pencil, mark the horizontal line across the stocking.

4 Select a piece of patterned fabric approx. 10 x 16cm (4 x 6½in). I used part of a panel showing Father Christmas. Lay the fabric right side up on the wadding and pin in place.

5 Take another strip or piece of fabric and lay it on top of the first one, right sides and one edge together. Stitch in place using a 5mm (¼in) seam allowance. Open out the two fabrics and finger press the top one to one side and pin in place.

6 Put another piece of fabric on top of the first two right sides together, taking care to cover the seam completely (see diagram).

7 Continue adding fabric in this way until you have covered the stocking up to the horizontal line. (It should cover the line but doesn't need to be exact.)

8 Place the strip of lace along the line and tack (baste) into place.

9 Place the straight edge of the white on white fabric right side down, just above the top edge of the lace and sew in place using a 5mm (¼in) seam allowance.

10 Cut toe and heel pieces from one of your selected prints using Templates B and C on page 126, and adding a 5mm (¼in) seam allowance to the straight sides. Press the seam allowance to the wrong side on the straight edges.

11 Pin the heel in position on the stocking and topstitch along the straight edges. Pin the toe piece in position and topstitch the straight edge.

12 Tack (baste) all round the outside edge of the stocking front holding the heel and toe and the edges in place from the wrong side. Trim to the exact shape and size of Template A on page 126. If you wish, you can cover the seams with machine embroidery using the gold thread.

13 Lay the fabric for the stocking back face down with the wadding (batting) and lining on top. Tack (baste) all round the edges and trim the wadding (batting) to the exact shape and size of Template A.

14 Bind the top of each half of the stocking (see Binding, page 9). Bind all around the stocking, using the binding seam to join the two halves together. Leave a length of binding hanging in the top corner diagonally opposite the toe.

15 Hand hem the other edge of the bias binding down. Oversew the edges on the loose binding at the top, tuck the end in and hem stitch it closed. Thread a curtain ring for hanging the stocking onto the binding and stitch the end down to the lining inside the stocking.

YOU WILL NEED

- Plain green or red lining fabric, 1m (1yd)
- White on white fabric, 25cm (¼yd)
- Waste fabric, 50cm (½yd) (as background for crazy patchwork)
- 2oz wadding (batting), approx. 1m (1yd) square
- White lace, approx. 30cm (12in)
- Scraps of Christmas or red, green or gold print fabrics for crazy patchwork
- Red, green or gold print fabric, 50cm (½yd) for back of stocking
- Green or red bias binding, 2.25m (2½yds) by 2.5cm (1in)
- Gold machine embroidery thread (optional)
- One white plastic or brass curtain ring

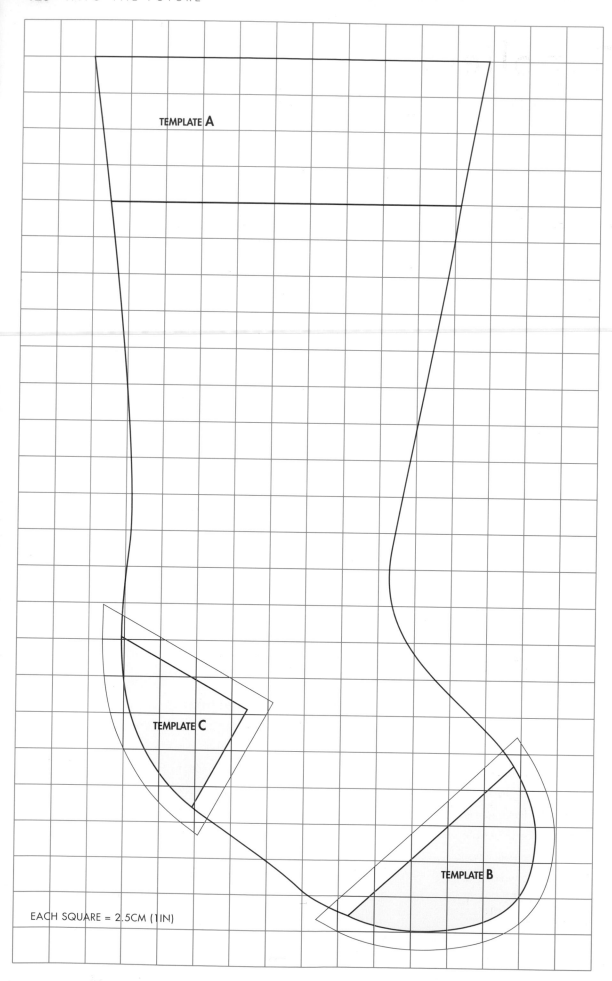

TEMPLATE A

TEMPLATE C

TEMPLATE B

EACH SQUARE = 2.5CM (1IN)

Suppliers

The Bramble Patch
West Street
Weedon
Northants
NN7 4QU
Tel/Fax: 01327 342212
*Fabrics, including Kunin felts, equipment,
threads etc.*

Diane Dorward
27 Hawkwood Close
Malvern
Worcs
WR14 1QU
Tel/Fax: 01684 564056
E-mail: diane.dorward@virgin.net
*Stencils, paint and brushes, template plastic,
rag rugging tools and hessian.
Send SAE for catalogue*

Quiltlets Ltd.
Garden Cottage
Rowfold
Billingshurst
West Sussex
RH14 9DD
Tel: 01403 783696
E-mail: fjs-rowfold@compuserve.com
Professional machine quilting service

Strawberry Fayre
Chagford
Devon
TQ13 8EN
Tel: 01647 433250
Fabrics by mail order

White Cottage Country Crafts
24 Post Office Road
Seisdon
Wolverhampton
West Midlands
Tel: 01902 896917
Fabrics, equipment, threads etc.

Acknowledgements

This has been a long and arduous labour of love, since the book was started before and completed after I had brain surgery. The first part was so easy compared to the second. Many times I have wanted to throw it in because I haven't got the speed, concentration or memory I once had. Thanks are due to Cheryl Brown, Brenda Morrison and David & Charles for their long suffering patience, my friends and family for their encouragement and especially Robert, my husband for his firm and unstinting support. Thanks to Honeychurch Toys of Devizes, for supplying all the toys for the book's photography.

Thanks also to Avril Hopcraft, for her support across the distance, friendship and brilliant sewing; to Di Dorward who keeps me going, makes me laugh and is a true friend and to Barbara Chainey for sound advice, practical help and for always being on the end of the phone. This one is due to you lot!

Index

Page numbers in *italics* refer to illustrations, those in **bold** refer to diagrams and those in brackets refer to templates